Trout Fishing In The Shenandoah National Park

Trout Fishing In The Shenandoah National Park

By Harry W. Murray

Introduction by Charles F. Waterman

Photographs by the author

Shenandoah Publishing Company

ISBN 0-9622555-0-5

Printed in the United States of America by Good Printers, Bridgewater, Virginia 22812.

Cover design by William J. Didawick.

Cover photograph by the author.

This book is dedicated to my children—Milly, Nicki, Liz, Jeff and Susan.

ACKNOWLEDGEMENTS

I am deeply indebted to many people who have helped tremendously in the preparation of this book; without their assistance it could not have been written. These are listed alphabetically.

Tim Alley, Bill Burslem, Jim Dexter, Bill Didawick, William Downey, Shawn Green, David Haskell, Dave King, Jeff Murray, Susan Murray, Glenn Morrison, Dick Rabun, Gerald Racey, Clinton Runyon, George Sheetz, Susan Smith, Terri Tisinger, Bill Wade, Bob Warren, Charley Waterman, Debie Waterman.

Other book by author: Fly Fishing For Smallmouth Bass.

CONTENTS

A Message From The Superintendent
Of Shenandoah National Park

Shenandoah National Park offers one of the few large areas of wild trout habitat in the eastern United States. Each year millions of Americans visit this great national park seeking a chance to enjoy its many natural and cultural resources. Located only a short distance from the nation's capital and other large metropolitan areas Shenandoah provides opportunities for many people. At the same time, management challenges in the protection of these resources sought after by so many are ever present.

Wild brook trout are but one of the outstanding natural resources we as park managers are charged with protecting. However, it is important to mention that game fish are the only species of wildlife in the Park that, by law, visitors are allowed to harvest or even disturb in any way. Because of this, brook trout populations must be managed carefully in order to assure their long term viability.

The Park's Fisheries Management Plan objectives for native trout management in Shenandoah National Park are twofold: (1) To preserve and perpetulate the native brook trout as an integral component of the Park's aquatic ecosystems and (2) to allow for recreational angling. Meeting these objective requires careful management and the full cooperation of the angling public. You, as anglers and conservationists, can help to assure that trout populations remain healthy and that the outstanding angling opportunities that now exist continue into the future. Beyond obeying the regulations and being good sports persons, I encourage you, whenever possible, to foster the catch-and-release angling concept, especially in heavily fished streams. This will allow other visitors to have the experience of catching the fish that are released. Handle fish that are to be released carefully to avoid injuring them, and be a good example to other anglers that you encounter on the stream. By doing these things you will have a lasting positive effect on the well being of this precious resource.

If you observe violations of any park regulations please report your observations to the nearest Ranger station or call Park Headquarters as soon as you can. (703) 999-2227.

My staff and I wish you many memorable outdoor experiences during your visits to the Park, and that you will be able to return often.

INTRODUCTION
By Charles F. Waterman

Harry Murray is one of the world's best trout fishermen, and although such a distinction may never make him famous outside trout angling circles, I don't think anyone will dispute it. He became what he is by fishing for trout, studying them, teaching about them and listening to other expert anglers.

I think you'd better read this little note about Murray before flipping through his book. One of the most important things about his text is that it is aimed at a specific area with which he is familiar. He wouldn't write about any kind of fishing he hadn't studied thoroughly, and if you are looking for a package of generalities this is the wrong place. He not only knows trout but he has spent years teaching and guiding trout fishermen and Harry Murray is not a secret keeper. His philosophy is that a serious trout angler deserves the information.

So we're dealing with a lifelong angling addict (there are snapshots of Harry Murray working at it as a pre-schooler) as well as a professional guide, master fly tyer, one-on-one teacher and author of many articles stressing the how-to of trout catching. I guess we can say he's the expert's expert and some very fine anglers are among his students—but he keeps learning from them too, which he seems to feel is the name of the game.

Harry Murray tied up a bunch of unnamed flies that copied some strange little bugs that strayed across his desk from a nearby stream and they caught trout. I have seen him stand in deep, fast water casting huge flies for big fish and I have seen him catching small brook trout while kneeling in a hard rainstorm by a tiny creek. He has been there and keeps going back.

CHAPTER 1
TROUT FOOD

As a prospective trout angler in the Shenandoah National Park is it important to have an understanding of the various foods upon which these trout feed? Well, yes and no; there are three ways to approach this.

If you are not interested in the many natural trout foods, and figure your persuasive powers with a fly rod are greater than the trout's will to resist your offerings, you need not delve deeply into the matter. The same fly your brother did well with in Montana, or the one the neighbor's son took all those bluegills on last summer, might do the job on the Park's brook trout. Strangely enough, this casual approach often works; a problem arises, however, when an artificial fly, selected in this manner, fails to catch trout.

Without, at least, some basic understanding as to why this fly pattern had previously been readily accepted by the trout, it is very difficult to know which fly to use when it fails. In most cases, anglers who accept this approach simply go through a trial and error process to find a fly the trout will take. Unfortunately, by the time they have gone through their entire fly box and found the fly which works, it is about time to call it a day. And, worst of all, they do not really know why the last fly was accepted by the trout, so they are unable to draw on this day's valuable lesson for future situations. There was a reason the trout accepted the first fly and, quite obviously, they later had a preference for the last fly, but do you know why? Most probably, your analysis of situations like this will directly affect your success on future trips.

A second approach to evaluating the natural foods upon which the trout feed is simply to be observant of what is going on about you when you are on the streams.

For example, you see several trout sipping cream colored natural flies from the stream's surface. You attach a size 14 Light Cahill dry fly to your leader and have fantastic fishing all day.

There is absolutely nothing wrong with this approach. It was the system used by my tutor in these mountains many years ago, and since Jack Sperry probably caught more trout here than any other angler ever has or ever will, I know the system works. Jack always said, "If you want to be consistently successful in catching trout in the Park, try to duplicate what Nature is doing."

William Downey checks the natural insects in the stream because he feels, "If you want to be consistently successful in catching trout in the Park, you should try to duplicate what Nature is doing."

The factor which put the odds on Jack's side with his approach was that he was always extremely observant and seldom missed a thing. This, plus the fact that he had a half-century of angling experience in these mountains, enabled him to take trout under almost any condition.

By being keenly aware of what is happening on the stream and carefully linking this with previous experiences under similar conditions, you can be quite successful in your fishing. The degree of your success will depend upon the keenness of your observations and the validity of your analysis.

The third approach to the trout food in the Park is based on actually utilizing the information gained in the last system (observation) and blending this with some careful studying. Don't run away; I am not implying that you need four years of entomology and three years of Latin to catch trout in the Park.

The mere suggestion of this has deprived many would-be trout anglers of a lifetime of joy. This stage is not required and, in some cases, is not even desired. Some fishermen are extremely well versed in textbook entomology and ichthyology, and yet couldn't catch a wise old brookie if you put it in their boot. The textbook study must be combined with actual stream and food evaluations to be meaningful.

"After spending almost a full year on the stream bottom . . . the Quill Gordon nymph will pop his wings and swim to the surface."

For example, reading how the March Brown Nymphs move to the sides of the Horse Brook Run section of the Beaverkill in New York may actually confuse you here in the Park. That section of the Beaverkill is about two hundred feet long; few pools in the Shenandoah National Park streams are twenty feet long. Where should I look in these small streams to locate these nymphs? How far will the trout pull out to feed on them? When do I look for them, and most of all, how do I fish this situation? Keen stream observations will answer these questions, but I will also cover this in the following pages.

A brief look at the life cycles of the major aquatic insects in the Park is helpful in understanding how the trout feed upon them.

Evaluating how the various insect stages alter this is not confusing, since the majority of this food source is represented by a relatively small number of flies. For example, only six different mayflies represent approximately 80 percent of the food load of this popular fly in the Park streams. And, the significant caddisflies and stoneflies have fewer numbers than the mayflies.

Since most anglers on these streams are concerned primarily with the mayflies, a look at their life cycles may be helpful.

After spending almost a full year on a stream bottom, the nymph prepares to leave the stream as the dun (subimago). This may be done by either swimming to the surface in the nymph form, or, as in the case of the Quill Gordon, by popping his wings on the stream bottom and swimming to the surface.

Once the surface is reached, the fly rids himself of the nymph case and rides along on top of the water, while drying his wings. At this point many of the duns fly from the stream to the foliage on the banks. Some, however, flop and skate along until they reach the bank, whereupon they rest and completely dry their wings; then these flies also head for the foliage.

One or two days is spent here, depending on the specific fly. During this stage the dun sheds his dull attire and becomes the completed adult spinner (imago) capable of reproducing. The spinners fly back over to the stream where they meet to perform the impressive "mayfly dances." After mating here, the females deposit the eggs into the stream and shortly thereafter die. The males die soon thereafter, and both fall to the stream surface as the spent spinner.

The eggs settle to the stream bottom where they become securely attached. After maturing, the nymph emerges and grows, with many moltings, until approximately one year later, when he emerges as a dun and the cycle starts again.

The caddisflies and stoneflies have similar cycles, and each have their own characteristics. Some caddisflies live for several weeks in the adult form, presenting an extended feeding period to the trout. The Giant Stonefly Nymphs are in the streams for several years before hatching, so the trout will always have a variety of sizes of this insect.

4

My stream notes show that the dates of the emergence of these insects vary considerably from year to year. Some theories suggest this is influenced primarily by the amount of light reaching the stream, but this has not been my observation. I find that the water temperature is the primary physical factor influencing the time of emergence of the Park's aquatic insects.

Once the stream's water temperatures reach 40 to 45 degrees Fahrenheit the flies start hatching. The sequence follows that shown in the following chart, but there is often a fair amount of overlap. It is not at all unusual to have Quill Gordons, Blue Quills and March Browns all on the water at the same time.

Mayflies

The following, unless otherwise specified, is compiled from notes of my experiences in the Park over the last twenty-eight years. The dates of the emergences of various aquatic insects are averages. Only food forms which are found in significant quantities in a number of Park streams will be covered, unless otherwise noted. For example, the much-loved Green Drake is not

This March Brown mayfly was one of the insects the author was attempting to imitate when he designed the Mr. Rapidan Dry fly.

present on all streams, and even where he is found, his numbers are not great. Most trout in the Park live their entire lives without ever seeing a Green Drake.

When I started fishing the Park in 1960, there was no dependable information on the identification and distribution of aquatic insects in these streams. At the encouragement of many anglers, and, with invaluable assistance of Art Flick, the major hatches were identified. The texts used for this are by Dr. Barnard Burks and Dr. Donald DuBois. The distribution study is still ongoing, not so much to determine which insects are located in specific streams, since I have been doing this for so long, but to observe the influences of various biological and physical factors upon acquatic insect population densities. I have found this information quite useful in anticipating the growth, and thus the potential sizes, of specific age classes of trout on certain streams. Factors such as drought, streambed scouring, adverse climatic conditions, and excessively full streams at the time of egg deposit, all can have an adverse effect upon insect population densities.

Throughout this discussion I will use the popular names known by anglers for specific insects and minnows, although, where I feel it is of value I will provide the scientific names.

Major Mayfly Hatches In The Shenandoah National Park

Insect	Mar.	Apr.	May	June	July	Anglers Name	Artificial Dry	Artificial Nymph
Epeorus pleuralis	▓					Quill Gordon	Quill Gordon 12, 14 Mr. Rapidan 12, 14	Quill Gordon 12, 14 Mr. Rapidan 12, 14
Paraleptophlebia adaptiva		▓				Dark Blue Quill	Blue Quill 16, 18	Blue Quill 16
Stenonema vicarium			▓			March Brown	March Brown 12, 14 Mr. Rapidan 12, 14	March Brown 12, 14
Stenonema fuscum			▓			Grey Fox	Grey Fox 14 Ginger Quill 14	Grey Fox 14 March Brown 14
Stenonema canadense			▓			Light Cahill	Light Cahill 14 Grey Yellow N. H. 16	Light Cahill 14
Ephemerella dorothea				▓	▓	Sulphur	Fox Sulphur 16, 18 Grey Yellow N. H. 16, 18	Sulphur 16, 18 Phesant Tail 16, 18

Caddisflies & Stoneflies

Caddisflies and stoneflies are often overlooked by anglers in the Park.

In the case of the caddisflies, this probably results from the lack of selectivity exhibited by trout when they are feeding on the natural adult flies. In addition to the three caddisflies listed on the following chart, there are several others present in less dense populations. However, an Elk Hair Caddis usually does the job when the tent-winged naturals are over the water.

"Charles Brooks' concept of tying the caddis larva 'in the round' produces an especially productive pattern _____ ."

The underwater forms of the caddis should not be brushed over lightly, especially the larva form of the Rhyacophlila. This "naked larva" is readily available to the trout over a fairly long time period, and the absence of a larva case apparently makes him a tempting meal. This is one of the "little green worms" we all see on the stream bottom.

Charles Brooks' concept of tying these larva "in the round" produces an especially productive pattern wherever they are found.

The two stoneflies shown on the following chart are the most significant ones, as far as duplicating them from an angling point of view is concerned.

The Little Yellow Stonefly is present for the time span shown, but what I could not show is the density of the hatch.

During some years these flies are present in unbelievably large numbers, prompting the trout to feed heavily on them for months. Residing in leaves and other soft bottom materials, the Isoperla Nymphs are quite susceptible to floods. For example, there were very sparse hatches of these stoneflies during the summer of 1986; as anticipated, the heavy flood waters in November of 1985 had taken a heavy toll.

The other major stonefly, the Giant Stone, was not affected as drastically by the flood. He lives under larger, more stable rocks, and being much larger, was better equipped for the flood.

Anglers should remember that the multi-year cycle means there are always some Giant Stonefly Nymphs in the stream.

Don't be tricked into thinking you will have a field day when the honest size 6 adults are about the stream. I love to fish the large drys during a similar hatch in Montana, but the manner of emergence of these flies (the nymphs crawl out onto dry land), and the low stream conditions during the summer prevent the brookies from going on a feed. I've seen dozens of these giant adults flop clumsily on low clear pools without drawing even a splashy rise from a trout.

There are some good hatches of Tiny Dark Early Stoneflies in the Park, but the fish are not selective when feeding upon them. Often, in fact, the streams are so high when these flies are on, the fish don't seem to know the flies are up there.

The following chart shows when the various caddisfly and stonefly hatches occur and fly effective fly patterns.

Major Caddisfly And Stonefly Hatches In The Shenandoah National Park

Insect	April	May	June	July	Aug.	Sept.	Anglers Name	Artificial Dry Fly	Artificial Nymph
Brachycentrus (Caddisfly)	▨	▨					American Grannom	Elk Hair Caddis Olive 14, 16	Olive Pupa 14
Rhyacophlila (Caddisfly)			▨	▨			Green Sedge	Elk Hair Caddis Olive 14, 16	Green Larva 14
Pycnopsyche Caddis (Caddisfly)						▨	Brown Sedge / Stick Bait (local)	Elk Hair Caddis Brown 14, 16	Brown Pupa 12, 14
Isoperla bilineata (Stonefly)		▨	▨	▨	▨		Yellow Sally / Little Yellow Stonefly	Little Yellow Stonefly 16, 18 Light Goofus 16	Red Squirrel Nymph 16 / Little Yellow Stonefly 16
Pteronarcys dorsata (Stonefly)	▨	▨	▨				Giant Black Stonefly	Improved Sofa Pillow 6	Brooks Dark Stonefly Numph 8, 10

Terrestrial Insects

Terrestrial insects represent a very large part of the diet for the trout in the Shenandoah National Park.

The timing of their appearances dovetails nicely with reduction in densities of aquatic insects. There is definitely some overlap in the seasonal appearances between aquatic and terrestrial insects. However, during the summer and fall, when sizeable aquatic insects are scarce, many of the land-born insect populations are at their peaks.

Surprisingly little attention has been given to fishing fly patterns which duplicate these flies in small mountain streams. Charlie Fox, a good friend, who coined the term "terrestrial flies," as they apply to the anglers, once told me that his favorite mountain trout fly was a Crowe Beedle.

The following chart is not meant to be a true hatch chart but, rather, is intended to show the seasonal distribution of specific terrestrial insects. The darkly shaded areas indicate the periods of greatest population densities, and the lighter sections show more sparse numbers. The fly sizes indicated represent the major ranges which occur. Specific fly pattern sizes to be fished on a certain day should be selected to match the natural insects along the stream. There are many other land-born insects in the Park, but most of the fly patterns listed will be accepted readily by the trout when other insects are present. For example, there are often periods when there are a fair number of two different wasps along the stream; Shenk's Crickets and Letort Hoppers are very effective when the insects are present.

Terrestrial Insects In The Shenandoah National Park

Insect	April	May	June	July	Aug.	Sept.	Oct.	Fly Pattern
Black Ants								Black Fur Ant 12-20 Black McMurray Ant 14-22 Black Flying Ant 14-20
Cinnamon Ants								Cinn. Fur Ant 14-18 Cinn. McMurray Ant 14-22
Beetle								Crowe Beetle 10-18
Inchworms								Inchworm 12-14
Crickets								Shenk's Cricket 10-16
Grasshoppers								Letort Hopper 12-16 Dave's Hopper 10-14
Leaf Hopper								Jassids 18-22

Miscellaneous Foods

The Park's trout have not lasted this long by being stupid; they will feed on almost any natural insect which comes within view. They could care less whether or not it fits nicely into our organized systems of grouping and identifications.

Some of these insects are far more important at certain seasons than others, and some are much more prevalent on certain streams than others.

For example, the natural Crane Fly Larva are readily taken quite early in the season by the trout on some of the largest streams. Realizing the streams are often rather high at this time of the year, I developed a special pattern which would look, and fish, like the real larva. I taught one of my regular fly tying classes at Lord Fairfax College how to tie this fly; from that time on it has been the number one pattern for these, and other, serious early season anglers.

These larva look much like grubs; they are a translucent creamish-tan and range from one-half to one inch long.

Fish Fly Larva can be important on some streams especially when other major aquatic insects groups are absent.

The Chironomidae are very numerous on many Park streams. Many anglers refer to these simply as midges.

They are most significant from an angling point of view in the fall. The trout feed well on the pupa at that time and even take the adult drys when they can get them. Size 22 Olive or Black Midges, fished delicately over working trout, will produce good action in the low, flat pools in September.

I have seen trout stuff themselves on midge larva and pupa in protected eddies in the spring, but they are seldom selective. I've had no trouble taking these fish on larger nymphs, and since the hooking percentages are less on size 22 nymphs, I seldom go after them this way.

Trout feed well on natural Crawfish since each one represents a lot of groceries. These are available to the fish primarily late in the evenings and when the water is slightly discolored. Full, discolored streams, in fact, are the best time to fish these imitations. A size 8 Squirrel Tail Crawfish is effective at these times, but it is a little more fly than we want in normal conditions.

Minnows

There are many different minnows throughout the Park, and there are very heavy populations in some streams. The trout definitely feed on them, but fly patterns and lures duplicating them are most effective with high and discolored stream conditions.

Certainly, it is possible to tie the popular streamer patterns in very small sizes and take trout on them under normal water conditions, but slapping a size 8 Mickey Finn into a low, flat pool will scare the spots off the trout. Even when the mini-streamers are effective in the Park they usually don't produce as many strikes as the properly selected dry flies or nymphs.

The following was provided by the Shenandoah National Park.

Minnows In The Shenandoah National Park

Blacknose Dace-Rhinichthys atratulus
Longnose Dace-Rhinichthys cataractae
Redside Dace-Clinostomus funduloides
S. Redbelly Dace-Phoxinus erythrogastor
Mtn. Redbelly Dace-Phoxinus oreas
Bluehead Chub-Nocomis leptocephalus
River Chub-Nocomis micropogon
Common Shiner-Notropic cornutus
Creek Chub-Semotilus atromaculatus
Common Stoneroller-Campostoma anomalum
Cutlips Minnow-Exoglossum maxillingua
Fantail Darter-Etheostoma flabellare
Johnny Darter-Etheostoma nigrum
Tessellated Darter-Etheostoma olmstedi
Mottled Sculpin-Cottus bairdi
Margined Madtom-Noturus insignis

CHAPTER 2

TACKLE

The fishing tackle which works well in the Park overlaps that used in other areas to a certain extent, but there are refinements which one can make that improve the odds and enhance the sport.

For example, the vest, hat, hippers, and assorted gadgets are the same ones I use on Pennsylvania's limestone streams and Montana's spring creeks, but the rods are different in some cases. However, the same rods I use on the Park's small streams work quite well on the headwater streams in the Green Mountains of Vermont, the Smokies in North Carolina, and the Crazy Mountains in Montana.

By selecting the correct tackle in the beginning many frustrations and disappointments can be prevented, and this wonderful endeavor will be extremely rewarding.

Fly Tackle

Fly rods: The demands for accurate fly placement and a delicate presentation set the ground rules for rod selection in the park. This is further complicated by the fact that we need to achieve these goals at relatively close range.

I have many fly rods of various lengths which are capable of startling accuracy at thirty feet and beyond, but they are very disappointing at the honest fifteen to twenty foot ranges needed in the park. I simply can't hit what I'm shooting at with them. Basically, what we are looking for is a rod with a delicate tip and a moderately fast butt which balances with a number 2, 3, or 4 fly line.

Fly rods requiring size 5 and larger lines seldom perform well on these small streams, especially since most rods are constructed with graphite today. Few of these rods will flex adequately with ten to twenty feet of line to give the accuracy needed, and over-lining them for proper loading robs us of a delicate presentation.

The overhanging tree limbs on these small streams definitely limit the length of the rod that can be safely used. It can be very upsetting to chop into a low tree limb on your forward cast and suddenly realize that you just converted

13

"We are looking for a rod from 7 to 8 feet long which will balance with a 2, 3, or 4 weight line and give accuracy and delicacy at close range."

your new two-piece rod into a three-piece rod by snapping off six-inches of the tip. Most mountain anglers like rods which range from 7 to 8 feet long.

I use several rods shorter than 7 feet long, but I find that I often spook the trout by moving in close enough to control the line on the water with these rods. They cast beautifully and do a fine job of delivering the fly, but the problem occurs once the line is on the water. I often think of what Joe Brooks, Virginia's most famous angler, told me about rod lengths in these small streams; Joe said, he did not know of anything that could be done with a rod less than 7½ feet long that couldn't be done better with one which was this length. On the other hand, rods more than 8 feet long just seem to be in the trees too much.

To summarize, we are looking for a rod from 7 to 8 feet long which will balance with a 2, 3, or 4 line and give accuracy and delicacy at close range.

Fly reels: At the first glance the fly reel does not appear to be a very demanding part of the Park angler's gear. However, observing a few simple rules will enable you to select a reel which will last a lifetime.

Most Park anglers prefer reasonably small, lightweight reels to balance with the light rods. Single action line recovery (where one turn of the reel handle recovers one wrap of line onto the spool) helps assure this light weight. Alloys and aluminum used in most modern reels provide us with a durable reel without adding excessive weight.

Durability and dependability are features we definitely want in a reel to be used in the back country. It is only a matter of time until you lose your footing on the slippery stream bottom and take a tumble.

Attempting to catch yourself by reaching down with your hands means the rod and reel will catch the full force of your body as you hit the deck. Under these circumstances I have bent reel spools, cracked frames, knocked handles off, and actually broken one reel completely in half. Eventually, one develops the reflex of gently tossing the rod and reel to the side during the fall; there is no time to aim for a soft landing spot for it, but at least you won't fall on it.

Dependability comes into play by assuring the reel will hold up under regular use. Here you may have to rely on the manufacturer's reputation. A better course is to talk to a number of anglers who have used the reel you are considering, and see how it has held up.

Having sold hundreds of reels by many manufacturers, since I've been in the fly shop business, here are some of the problems I've seen anglers encounter: screws lost from pillars, drag mechanisms fall out, center post become unscrewed, handles fall off, spools lock on center post and feet work loose. No accidents caused these problems; they just developed from normal use. Naturally, if you do much of your fishing in the remote areas of the Park, the odds are that you will encounter a problem here eventually and lose valuable fishing time.

The solution to this is either to carry an extra reel in your vest or invest in the best one you can find to meet your needs.

The drag should be adjustable and have the capacity to be set *very* lightly. The initial resistance of the drag, that point at which the first several inches of line are pulled from the reel, must be light enough to prevent a fish from breaking off on a light tippet when he "hits the reel." It makes little difference how smoothly the drag performs after twenty feet of line are peeled off, if the trout was lost before the first revolution of the spool was completed. This is seldom a problem in the Park, but when it does occur it may cost you the largest fish of the season.

Since it is quite probable that one would use this reel on other trout streams where larger fish are encountered, it is wise to be sure it has this capacity for a light starting drag.

Fly reels should be kept well oiled to assure smooth-running drags and free turning spools. They should be cleaned internally several times a season to prevent small particles of sand from grinding on the moving parts.

If you happen to drop your reel in the sand or dirt while fishing, immerse the whole reel into the stream and swish it back and forth several times to remove the dirt. If it still produces a grinding noise with each turn of the handle, remove the spool and rinse the frame and spool separately in the stream. The bath will not hurt your reel, but the sand will do permanent damage to it.

In testing prospective new reels for several manufacturers, one of the most common problems I encounter is having the fly line get in between the spool and the back of the frame. Reels which allow this to happen, even if it occurs only several times a season, should be avoided; this can ruin an expensive fly line.

Fly lines: Floating lines cover all the needs for Park trout fishing. Sinking tip lines, although helpful in other areas, are unnecessary here.

Both weight forward and double tapered lines work well, but since casts beyond thirty feet are seldom required the weight forward lines offer no advantage; however, the double tapered line gives the advantage of allowing you to reverse it when the first end is badly worn.

Proper line care will improve both the life and performance of any fly line. After every fifth trip I wash my line with a mild soap, rinse it, dry it, dress it with Mucilin or Glide, then wipe it dry. The last step here, wiping the dressing off the line, is very important. Dressing left on a line will pick up small dirt and grit particles. This will cause the tip of the line to sink eventually, but, worse, it acts like a miniature band saw blade. I saw a situation where permitting excessive dressing to remain on the line actually cut deeply into the guides of a new fly rod in one month, requiring complete guide replacements.

For many years I have converted my double tapered lines into what I call a "dry fly head." Using the first forty-feet of a double tapered line, I add fifty feet of twenty-five pound test Amnesia or Maxima monofilament with a needle knot, and apply three thin coats of Pliobond to the knot. This "dry fly head" is much like the floating shooting heads that Ted Trueblood popularized many years ago. However, I find that I can mend the casts more efficiently if the fly line is inside the tip of my rod than I can if I'm working with monofilment here. This "dry fly head" also provides economy by converting one double tapered fly line into two separate lines.

Dacron backing, behind the regular line or mono, helps fill the spool, permitting quick line recovery. If you plan to put a full double tapered fly line on your reel, a reasonable amount of backing will prevent the back portion of the line from crimping.

Leaders: It is extremely important to use the proper leader in order to achieve the accuracy in fly placement required on these small streams. Each year, when I conduct my fly fishing schools in the Shenandoah National Park, I find that the use of the wrong type leaders causes anglers more problems than any other single piece of their equipment. This is unfortunate when you consider that even the best leaders cost only about three dollars.

The best leaders I have found are those based on the Charles Ritz P. P. P. formulas. These call for moderately long butt sections, short mid sections and a medium length tippet section. This compound knotted leader provides latitude in design that will meet all the needs on small streams, including complete control of indicators for nymph and midge fishing.

Many anglers find that at these close ranges they lose accuracy with the flat butt, hinged butt, and braided butt leaders.

It is good insurance to carry a few extra leaders in your vest. I've seen fellows wrap their leaders around a tree limb in the back cast and rip the whole thing off trying to remove it.

I personally like to use a needle knot to attach my leader to the line, which I cover with three thin coats of Pliobond. There are other systems, but I've heard lots of horror stories concerning some of them. I want a knot I can trust!

Leader and tippet materials: This should be given all the consideration you give to your leaders. Whether you plan to build your own complete leaders or just add tippets and alter tapers on the streams, this is going to govern your efficiency in fly placement, drift control, natural fly action, and successful fish hooking. Yes, it is *extremely* important!

Factors you should consider are wet knot strength, resistance to curl, abrasion resistance, and flexibility.

The flexibility is going to determine if you can hit your target and obtain a realistic fly drift, and, if the other properties are reasonable, flexibility is the main aspect to consider in evaluating new leader materials. Mono which is either too stiff or too soft can cause a lot of problems.

Blood knots are the old standbys for connecting leader materials. They are still used for basic leader construction; however, the double or triple surgeons knots are much stronger and are preferred for connecting the tippet.

Indicators: The proper indicators will improve your catch with nymphs tremendously. There are many styles from which to choose; the best way to select the one which will serve you is to try them all and then settle on the one which meets your specific requirements.

I did this and settled for the ones made by Scientific Anglers. These look like small sections of bright fly line. They slide onto the leader and are held in place by the leader knots. Not only are these highly visible on the water's surface, but if I run my nymphs through very deep holes they can be seen far below the water. These cast quite well; in fact, several can be used at one time. Bill Burslem, a very efficient nymph fisherman, often uses three of these on one leader to provide complete control of strike detection, no matter what level he is fishing his nymphs.

17

Some of the squeeze-on styles provide good strike detection, but often float too well to let the nymphs run as deep as you might want them, thus requiring constant adjustments.

There are several slide-on styles made of cork and plastic which are so large they interfere with smooth casting and accurate nymph placement.

If I use one indicator, I normally place it three feet above the nymph; a second one is sometimes placed a foot above that one. If real shallow water is being fished I will often slide the first indicator down closer to the fly.

Fall midge fishing, even though these flies are floating, can be improved with indicators. These tiny flies can be very difficult for the angler to see on the water; by placing a quarter inch section of a Scientific Anglers indicator about three feet above them, the eyes are guided right down to the fly.

In summary, I like an indicator that I can see, which does not impede good casting, and which I can quickly move up or down the leader.

The vest: When purchasing a new vest be sure to get one with pockets which will hold your favorite boxes. Pocket placement and sizes are not standard on vests so just be careful.

I want a vest which will hold up to rough treatment. Until I found the vest I'm now using I wore out one vest every year. This was frustrating because I was using the, reputed, best ones on the market. Durability without excessive weight is important.

Lots of pockets are not essential on a vest for Park fishing; just make sure it has a back pocket large enough to carry a raincoat. Yes, I found this out the hard way; I almost drowned once!

The small belt-type vest which fit around the waist are comfortable in hot weather. Most hold all of the boxes and gadgets needed; just be very sure they have a back pocket large enough for a raincoat.

Raincoats: If you plan to fish the remote parts of the Park this is a *must*. Be sure it stops the rain, not just slows it down, is long enough to reach well below the tops of your hip boots, and is small enough to fit into the back of your vest. Hypothermia is an honest threat early and late in the season in the Park, and getting soaked miles from your car is asking for it.

Wading gear: Chest high waders are needed only early in the season on the lower reaches of some streams, and even here hippers will get you by if you are careful.

Boot foot hip boots are by far the most popular wading gear for the Park. You can walk a reasonable distance in them to reach out of the way areas, and many feel they might help deflect a snake's strike. They should definitely have felt soles.

Some anglers like to use only felt sole wading shoes to wade wet after the streams warm up. This, in fact, works well when fishing the back country since walking is more comfortable with these than in hippers. During cold weather it is a simple matter to carry a pair of light stocking foot hippers in the back of your vest and pull these on when you reach the part of the stream you plan to fish.

I have found that the lower priced wading shoes do not hold up well under heavy use. I used to wear out three pair of these a year and finally purchased a better quality shoe, constructed of a man-made leather. I get about five years out of these, and their sturdy construction provides excellent foot protection and support.

It is important to have the hippers or shoes fit properly to prevent discomfort and blisters. Be sure to allow adequate space for the wader socks you plan to use. A medium weight wool sock over a light polypropylene sock is a good system to provide comfort and to insure longer life of the wool socks.

Fly boxes: Many of the metal and plastic boxes with various clips and foam strips are excellent for nymphs, wet flies, and streamers. However, most of these will damage fragile dry flies.

The best boxes I've found for drys are the moderately flexible, metal hinged styles with compartments at least three-fourths of an inch deep. The most popular boxes of this style are made by Dewitt. They make a variety of sizes to fit all size pockets.

Be careful not to get a box too large for a specific vest pocket; even though it may actually fit the pocket, if it is on the large size you may damage the zipper getting it in and out.

If you happen to drop a box of flies into the stream, or worse, fall in over your vest pockets, be sure to dump the flies out when you get home to let both the flies and the box dry. If you do not, although neither the hooks nor the box will rust, you will definitely have a mess the next time you go fishing.

Polarized sunglasses: This is one of the most important items in the Park angler's gear. Many fishermen assume these are primarily used in spotting trout. This is a great asset, but possibly a greater advantage they give the mountain trout anglers is the ability to read the water. Under most conditions these trout cannot be seen, so it is necessary to evaluate the stream bottom makeup and currents in order to determine where to cast the fly.

I like light greenish-yellow lens in preference to the darker shades. Heavy shading often produces many dark areas on these streams, and the light lens work best.

I personally feel polarized glasses are so valuable that, for the past fifteen years, I've always kept two pair in my vest as insurance against loss or breakage.

Hats: Park fishing is no Easter parade, so, although, there is nothing wrong with wearing a sporty looking hat, this should not be the primary consideration in its selection.

The main consideration should be for one which will work right along with the polarized glasses to aid in seeing things underwater. This is achieved by having a large bill which is a dark color underneath.

The proper hat should slow a drizzle, keep it off your glasses, and be small enough to fit under the hood of a raincoat if it starts pouring. Cowboy hats can cause a problem here.

Clippers and scissor pliers: These are quite helpful for many jobs, only one of which is cutting leader materials. Keep them small, and stay away from low quality items; good ones cost only a fraction more and will last much longer and work better. The ones I'm using must be fifteen years old.

It is convenient to attach these to the vest with a yo-yo type retractor reel.

Needle nose pliers: Most Park anglers fish with barbless hooks and find this tool the best way to mash down the hook barbs. They are also helpful in constructing some knots.

I hope you'll never need them for this, but I once had to use them to remove a deeply imbedded hook from a fellow's arm whose back cast had gotten a little low.

Hemostats, forceps, and tweezers: No, we're not going into brain surgery. These are used primarily for removing hooks from a trout's lip. Since these are often attached to the front of the vest with a retractor reel they should be kept as

Customize your tweezers and clippers in order to meet your specific needs. Tweezers enable you to gently remove your flies from the trouts' jaws without harming them.

as small as possible. Most anglers use the mini-forceps, but I personally prefer square-tipped tweezers; these are a little more delicate when removing small flies from a trout's jaw. They are also very helpful in digging a size 22 fly from the back corner of a fly box.

Hook sharpening stones & flies: The only stone with which I have ever been satisfied is an ultra-fine Arkansas pencil stone. Most stones are too large and too coarse for use on very small trout flies.

Very slim, ultra-fine files are excellent. I've been using one for years and would feel lost without it.

Be cautious with medium or coarse files; they will grind the hook away too quickly, and most are too large to use on small hooks.

Floatants: Silicone creams work fine on hair flies like Shenk's Cricket and Letort Hoppers, but liquid floatants are preferred on hackled flies. Silicone creams can easily mat hackles and defeat you. After waterproofing, a dry fly should remain bright and the hackles resilient.

Fly drying powders: These were pioneered years ago by Dr. Donald DuBois, a very good friend. They work quite well. Remember to rinse your fly well in the stream after landing a trout, and squeeze off the excess water before applying this powder.

Leader sinking compounds: These are basically surface active agents that enable the leader to break through the water's top-most molecular layer. They work, but they require frequent applications to do their jobs properly. Adding no appreciable weight to the leader, you must rely on the weight of the fly, or lead added to the leader, to reach very deep.

Leader weighting products: Shot, squeeze-on, twist-on, dab-on, loop-on, and paint-on lead products all help take the leader, and thus the fly, to the stream bottom. I personally like removeable split shot because they can be easily added and removed as the stream conditions dictate.

A rig that works properly in pools four feet deep may hang up too often when you get to a section of the stream with few pockets over two feet deep. This usually prompts the angler to move the nymph so quickly through the pockets that the trout won't take it. If you encounter this situation when using removeable split shot it is a simple matter to pop it off, enabling you to fish your nymph properly.

Knives: A small Swiss pocket knife with a screwdriver blade, along with the regular blades, is handy to have for many purposes. Instant reel repairs can be made properly, and if a rod tip gets broken you may have to cut off several inches to make the repair.

Rod repair kit: In a small Ziplock plastic bag I carry: several size tip tops, several size snake guides, ferrule cement and a butane lighter. This weighs little, takes up only a small amount of space, and can easily save a trip.

Wader patching kit: Again, a trip saver; this can be the conventional patch-and-glue type kit or the heat-melt-and-smear type. The latter is easier and faster to use, but it will not work on a large hole. I once had the hot cement melt all the way through a boot, as I quickly found out it wouldn't work on all materials.

First aid and snake bite kit: It is wise to have a few basic items in case of an accident. Don't carry the large, heavy plastic boxes most of these come in. Scrounging a few of the basics from around home and carrying them in a small Ziplock bag is all that is required. Throw in a small, shrill whistle in case you get down and need to attract attention.

Snake bite kits come in three basic types—suction, freezing, and antivenin. I used to carry the latter until my physician told me the horse serum might kill me quicker than the snake bite. The freeze type is good, but it is large and bulky (I keep mine in the Jeep). The suction type is carried by most Park anglers, the majority of whom readily admit they would be too flustered to use it properly if the need arose.

This might be good; many emergency room physicians feel that if one can get to a hospital in a reasonable period of time it is better to do nothing than to play amateur surgeon.

"Terrestrial insects represent a very large part of the diet for the trout in the Shenandoah National Park." The Crickets, Hoppers, Beetles and Ants above are excellent patterns.

Insect repellent: Some people seem to require this more than others. The creams containing a high percentage of D E E T are quite effective and are easy to carry. One word of caution; I once dissolved the varnish off my favorite bamboo rod by repeatedly allowing it to rest on my wrist which had insect repellent on it. Prompted by this, my son Jeff set up a demonstration for his grade school science fair that fall.

Using five different makes of fly lines and six different insect repellents, he showed that all of the repellents would destroy all of the fly lines; it was simply a matter of time. So, be careful.

Flashlights: A small waterproof flashlight, with fresh batteries, is a must. Anglers wanting to fish until the last flicker of daylight rely on them to see when changing flies. Before I started carrying a flashlight my fishing partner, William Downey, and I almost got into trouble.

We fished the middle reaches of a small stream until quite late, planning to follow the trail back up the mountain to our car parked beside the Skyline Drive. We had judged the distance poorly and lost the trail in the black dark, miles below the top of the mountain. Crashing through the brush, with no indication of where we should go except up the mountain, finally brought us out on the Skyline Drive. That was the last time I fished the Park without a flashlight.

Stream thermometers: These are useful but not essential. If you are catching fish you may not even think about the water temperature. If, however, you happen to be on the stream early in the spring or late in the fall, and you are not getting the trout up to dry flies, your thermometer may show you the problem. A quick finding of thirty-six degrees Fahrenheit tells you that you had better switch to nymphs.

If you are playing on-going games with insect activities, trout feeding habits, and stream physical conditions, as I am, a good stream thermometer is essential.

Landing nets: These are not necessary in the Park. Inexperienced anglers do more harm to small trout with nets than they do without them, and knowledgeable angers don't need them.

Canteens and water bottles: Always carry your drinking water rather than relying on drinking from the stream. The old axiom, "If it's good enough for the trout, it is good enough to drink," is foolish. Some of these streams contain Giardia lamblia, a microscopic parasite, which can make you quite ill.

Most fellows use a simple plastic bottle or flask which they carry in the back of their vest. Belt canteens are fine, but I find they get in the way when I'm fishing.

Tape measures and rulers: If you plan to keep any fish, you must measure them to be sure they meet the minimum legal size limit. If you only plan to boast about the size of your big trout, do not use a tape to measure them. They will always be larger if you measure them with your handspan or some magical spot on the fly rod which has a way of growing each time you relate the story.

Fall-in-bag: It is wise to have a complete change of clothes in the car just in case you fall in or get caught in a rain. Have a warmer jacket than you think you might need. This can be very comfortable if you've been wet very long, and if the weather is colder in the Park than anticipated you may need it when you start out fishing.

Fishing license: Have this with you on the stream. Park rangers will not let you go fishing simply because you have yours back in the car. A license can be purchased at several locations in the Park, or from local state license agents.

Flies: A list of productive Park flies will contain many old standbys used all over the country. Some are more consistent than others, and there are some flies developed especially for the Park which are extremely productive.

Seasonal water conditions, aquatic and terrestrial insect activities, and minnow populations should be considered in selecting the flies to be used on a specific day. Reflecting on the discussion in Chapter 1, we should strive to "duplicate what Nature is doing."

Jeff Murray carefully selects a dry fly to "duplicate what Nature is doing." Even at a young age, he has come to realize this approach is the most successful.

Flies For The Shenandoah National Park

Dry Flies	Nymphs & Wet Flies	Streamers
Quill Gordon 12-16	Dark Stonefly Nymph 8-10	Muddler Minnow 8-10
Mr. Rapidan 12-18	Casual Dress 8-12	White Marabou Muddler 8-10
Blue Quill 16-18	Murray's Hellgrammite 10-12	Black Marabou Muddler 8-10
March Brown 12-14	Prince Nymph 10-14	Mickey Finn 8-10
Grey Fox 14	Quill Gordon Nymph 12-14	Black Nose Dace 8-10
Light Cahill 12-18	Mr. Rapidan Emerger 10-14	Spuddler 8
Sulphur 16-18	Blue Quill Nymph 18	Shenk's Sculpin 8
Adams 12-18	March Brown Nymph 12-14	Whitlock's Sculpin 8
Coachman Trude 12-16	Light Cahill Nymph 12-16	Black Woolly Bugger 8-10
Olive Elk Hair Caddis 12-18	Hare's Ear Nymph 10-14	Olive Woolly Bugger 8-10
Brown Elk Hair Caddis 12-18	Sulphur Nymph 16	
Irresistable 12-14	Olive Caddis Pupa 14	
Royal Wulff 12-18	Brown Caddis Pupa 12-14	
Light Goofus 12-16	Green Caddis Larva 14	
Dark Goofus 12-16	Crane Fly Larva 10-14	
Crowe Beetle 12-18	Fish Fly Larva 10-14	
Black Fur Ant 12-20	Yellow Stonefly Nymph 16	
Cinnamon Fur Ant 14-18	Grey Fox Nymph 14	
Ginger Quill 14	Phesant Tail Nymph 14-18	
Black McMurray Ant 14-22	Red Squirrel Nymph 10-14	
Cinnamon McMurray Ant 14-18	Coachman Wet 12-14	
Black Jassid 18-22	Quill Gordon Wet 12-14	
Inchworm 12-14	Black Gnat Wet 12-14	
Black Flying Ant 14-20	Brown Hackle 12-14	
Dave's Hopper 10-14	Light Cahill Wet 12-14	
Letort Hopper 12-16	March Brown Wet 12-14	
Shenk's Cricket 10-16		
Grey Yellow No Hackle 16-18		
Grey Yellow Hair Wing— No Hackle 16-18		
Tiny Olive Midge 22-24		
Tiny Black Midge 22-24		

Spinning Tackle

Many of the items listed above are the same used with spinning tackle, but certain items should be discussed.

Spinning rods: These should be very flexible, ultra light rods from five to six feet long. The short casts and very light lures used in the Park present accuracy problems with the average U. L. spinning rods.

Spinning reels: Ultra light, open front reels loaded with two or four-pound test lines are the best for this type fishing. Keep them well filled to facilitate smooth casting with lures down to a thirty second of an ounce. It is convenient to carry an extra reel spool filled with a lighter or stronger line. This gives you more latitude in fishing, and if you happen to get a bad bird's nest on your first spool, and lose a lot of line, it is a simple matter to change to the second spool.

Spinning lures: Park regulations permit the use of lures with single hooks only, and on the fish-for-fun streams the hooks must be barbless. It is permissible to cut off the extra two hooks on treble hook lures, or you can remove them and replace them with a single hook. Where barbless hooks are required you can mash or file down the hook, or do both—just as long as you remove the complete barb from the hook.

Spinning Lures

Gold Mepps Spinner 0 and 00	Gold Rebel 1/16 oz.
Silver Mepps Spinner 0 and 00	Silver Rapala #5
Rooster Tail Spinner 1/16 oz.	Gold Rapala #5
Panther Martin Spinner 1/16 oz.	Super Duper 1/22 oz.
Eppinger Daredevil 1/32 oz.	Jigs 1/64-1/32 oz.

CHAPTER 3
READING THE WATER

This phase of the angling game, more than any other, will determine the extent of your success in trout fishing in the Park!

For our purposes *reading the water* involves a three stage approach.

The first stage requires an accurate identification of the feeding stations within each pool; these are specific locations to which the trout move when they desire to feed.

In order to simplify the determination of these areas, and to clarify the discussion of angling tactics in later chapters, I have assigned names to the different feeding stations.

There are six possible feeding stations in each pool, but few pools have them all; some pools have only two or three. The *primary feeding station* is the one holding the largest fish in each pool.

The second stage of reading the water is deciding exactly where to cast the fly in order for it to drift, naturally, to the trout holding on the feeding station.

To achieve this, the rate and direction of the current between the feeding station and the point of fly placement must be accurately evaluated. So, too, the current onto which the leader will fall must be evaluated. You want your fly to drift all the way to the trout just as if it were not attached to the leader.

When fishing nymphs, this is further complicated by the fact that unseen under-water currents must be judged, in addition to surface currents. Here, not only are the rate and direction of the drift important, but you should strive to have your nymph at, or close to, the same depth as the trout when it reaches the feeding station.

As important as the first two stages are, the third stage is even more so.

Selecting the exact spot to stand, as you make your cast, will determine whether or not you can successfully combine stages one and two, in order to catch the trout.

If you make your presentation from too far away, the many mixed currents onto which the line and leader falls will cause your fly to behave in an unnatural manner and *drag* over the fish. Not only will this dragging action prevent the trout from taking the fly on this presentation, but he will seldom take successive drifts, even if they are natural.

Moving in too close to the trout's feeding station will spook him, abruptly ending the game.

Understanding several factors concerning the trout and his food will help you understand why, and therefore where, specific feeding stations are selected.

These beautiful, mountain freestone streams do not contain an overabundance of food; in fact, in comparison to rich limestone spring creeks, the food volume is shockingly low. It is, however, enough for these trout to live and grow. They have learned to take advantage of every delicate morsel available to them, by being constantly on the lookout for food, once the water temperature bumps over 40 degrees. This constant vigil for food goes on from spring until fall, being interrupted only occasionally if they become stressed by low water conditions late in the summer.

The desire to feed constantly moves the fish to the feeding stations, but these areas are not selected by chance, nor are they chosen simply because a lot of food is going to drift by one specific location within the pool.

The force of the current must be evaluated, by the trout, before selecting a feeding station. I don't think they have gotten into computers to aid in selecting these feeding stations, but their instincts are very efficient at this.

Biologically, the trout cannot justify expending more energy to consume a specific goody than the food value he derives from it.

Blending these two factors, we then realize the trout will select a feeding station that will enable him to gain the greatest amount of food with the least amount of effort. Lazy? No, he just instinctively knows how to play the game.

From an angling point of view this means you should be on the lookout for locations where the trout gains some protection from the full force of the current, while remaining fairly close to it. He will seldom be in the heaviest water or dead currents; however, he may move into the latter areas under special conditions.

There are six different feeding stations on which a trout may locate. Since these streams are usually fished upstream, to prevent scaring the trout, a logical approach in identifying them is to start at the furthest downstream feeding station and proceed up through the pool.

The **lip** is the first feeding station located in the lower part of the pool. It is formed as a boulder or several large stones form a small dam over which the water flows as it leaves the pool.

Most of the insects drifting through the pool are funneled to the **lip**, and the damming stones afford a break in the current for the trout. They can lie immediately in front of these stones, and, by simply tilting upward, pick off any insect drifting by.

The **lip** is frequently the pool's primary feeding station and usually produces well for most anglers. The most common error made by fishermen, attempting to fish the **lip** of a pool, is fishing it from the wrong spot.

30

The accurate identification of specific feeding stations is very important to anglers in the Shenandoah National Park.

Obviously the **lip** must be fished by staying well below it, actually in the upper portion of the next pool downstream. If you select a casting position too far below it, the current will pull your leader as the fly drifts over the feeding station, producing an unnaturally fast dragging action. The trout will seldom take a fly behaving in this manner.

In order to compensate for this, the obvious solution is to approach the **lip** closer. This will allow you to "bridge the **lip**" as I call it. Bridging amounts to holding the rod tip high enough to keep the line and leader out of the fast current falling over the **lip**. This works very well in eliminating the undesirable drag, but if you move in too closely you will spook the trout.

The shorter the rod the closer you must move to the **lip** in order to prevent drag, so be careful of really short rods.

Each year, when I conduct my fly fishing schools in the Park, I find it necessary to work with most anglers, to help them determine the best casting position for fishing the **lip** and several other feeding stations where drag can easily occur. This is not difficult to learn, and by continually reminding the students to pause momentarily to evaluate the currents in the area of the feeding station, they pick it up quickly.

31

If you are starting to fish these streams on your own, the trout will be your instructors. The drag produced by fishing any feeding station from too far away, or with improper line handling, will prevent the trout from taking your fly. Often, you will see him pull up under it, only to have it snatched away at the last second by the current. By selecting a casting position too close to the feeding station, or by moving in too noisily, you will see the fish run up into the pool as you scare him. Not to worry; you are learning.

Take what you learn in each situation, whether you spook the fish or land him, and apply it to future situations. I have always felt these little mountain streams could teach observant anglers more than any other types of water. Each little pool is a new testing ground for what you have learned in the previous pools and on previous trips (and from this book).

I have friends who have become highly accomplished anglers, successfully fishing many of the finest and most demanding trout streams across the country, primarily because they learned well the basic lessons these Park streams can teach.

The **tail** of the pool, lying just upstream of the **lip**, is the next feeding station. It is seldom selected by the largest fish in the pool, but, on occasion, may be, if there is no distinct **lip** on the pool.

The water in this area eases out of the pool, rather than being abruptly halted as in the case of the **lip**. There is seldom a specific feature here which provides protection from the current for the trout. A slight change in the stream bottom, seen as a small pocket only inches deeper than the surrounding areas, often constitutes this feeding station.

Being rather inconspicuous, the exact location of this feeding station can be difficult to pinpoint. This produces a temptation for anglers to cover the entire area in a shotgun style casting, flipping flies all across the **tail** and hoping, through luck, that one drift will be over the trout. This logic goes hand-in-hand with the desire to fire numerous casts all the way up into the **head** of the pool, and hope that somewhere along the way a trout will see the fly and take it. Nothing could be worse!

It is highly unlikely that casts directed in this manner will produce many fish; more than likely drag will set in, ruining the drift by the time the trout sees the fly.

Unfortunately, this cast-and-hope approach occasionally produces a trout, prompting the angler to assume he is using the correct tactic. Here, instant success may result in ultimate failure, since the art of **reading the water** may never be mastered.

A better system is to analyze the water, select the exact spot where you expect the trout to be holding, and accurately cast your fly a foot or two above him. If you are correct, you catch your fish, and you know you are learning. If you do not get him, you are still learning. You now know you read the set up

William Downey detected "a small pocket only inches deeper than the surrounding area" which formed a good feeding station in the **tail** *of this pool."*

wrong, incorrectly identifying the feeding station and dropping the fly at the wrong spot. Reflecting on these inaccurately read setups (and we all have many of them) will help you read them correctly in the future. You are learning!

The **mid-pool,** lying a short distance above the **tail** of the pool station, is the next feeding station upstream.

This is the largest portion of the pool and receives the greatest amount of attention from beginning anglers. It provides a big target, is easy to fish, and lets you work a longer line than any other part of the pool. It is unfortunate this presents such a tempting situation because it is one of the least productive feeding stations, primarily producing young fish. The dinks are here because the larger fish will not permit them to hold on the better feeding stations.

Lack of protection from the current is the primary reason larger trout seldom feed here. Often the only stream-slowing features occur on the stream bottom, and, through a natural adaptation process, the trout have learned this is not the best way to feed. Swimming from the stream bottom to the surface, through three or four feet of water, can burn more energy than the food value derived from the insect, depending on the rate of the current.

Still, make an attempt to identify the specific lies within the **mid-pool** area, and run your flies through them. Stay well below the main part of the pool while fishing this area to prevent scaring the trout. If the water is excessively fast in the **tail,** and you must move around it to prevent drag, you should go in low and fish the **mid-pool** area from your knees so the trout won't see you.

The **head** of the pool is an easily identified feeding station, but selecting the spot to drop the fly requires some thought.

In this case these brookies may trick you; they have their own set of values concerning exactly where to locate around white water.

If you are a first time angler in the Park, having cut your teeth on the rainbows in the Smokies in North Carolina, you may be surprised to find the brook trout here seldom hold in the heavy water your rainbows did.

If you learned your angling tactics from the cutthroat trout in Pelican Creek in the Yellowstone country, you will invariably make many wasted cast into slow water to the sides of the **head** of the pool. The Park's brookies don't like this any more than they do the real heavy white water.

There are, of course, exceptions to this, but if the water onto which you are dropping your flies fails to produce, you must adjust your tactics.

The Park's trout seek out the edges of the white water. In teaching my classes, I encourage the students to drop their flies "where the fast water meets the slow water" as Dan Bailey often directed.

This narrow buffer line, along both sides of the incoming riffle, should produce a fish or two in each pool. Be careful with your aim; a dry fly which lands in the heavy white water can drag quickly. A nymph dropped too far up

34

into the heavy current may race around the main part of the leader, depriving you of knowledge of the strike when it occurs.

The **back eddy** is the next feeding station to consider. Depending on the physical makeup of the pool it may be desirable to fish this before you move to the **head**. It's about fifty-fifty. The trout will let you know if you did it properly because, here, they can be very tricky.

Anglers fall into one of three categories concerning **back eddies**; some are fascinated with them because of the challenges they present; others are frustrated with them for the same reasons; and a third group gives them little thought because they do not realize what goes on in them.

Back eddies are formed as an extra amount of water, in a specific pool, cannot empty across the **tail** as fast as the main current. The main flow produces a damming effect, which turns this extra volume to the side, often flowing *away* from the lower part of the pool. Beginning anglers occasionally refer to these currents as flowing upstream. Naturally, it is not flowing uphill, but one portion of a **back eddy** will flow in the opposite direction of the main stream currents.

Think of a **back eddy** as a very slow-moving whirlpool with a flat surface. It may range from two to twenty-feet wide.

Debie Waterman fights a nice brook trout in the Park. She found many similarities between reading the water on these brook trout streams and her cutthroat trout streams in Montana.

If it's so slow why would a trout choose to feed here? What about needing all that food the current must bring him? That's a good point, but look at the mechanics of a big **back eddy.**

It serves as a collecting bowl for all type insects. The surface layer is incredibly slow to leave and join the main current in the pool. This produces a giant lazy Susan which serves the insects up to the waiting trout again and again and again. In mid-April I've seen dozens of Blue Quill mayflies, too chilled to make a rapid exit, riding around and around in a single **back eddy,** presenting easy pickings for the waiting trout.

Yes, waiting, holding in some slight depression or beside an almost obscure rock, rising to delicately sip off each fly in turn, as it drifts by. You see, he doesn't have to exert much energy, and the odds are, that the majority of food in the **eddy** will eventually drift right into his dining room.

As you will see in the chapter on tactics, the **back eddy** is at its best under some very special conditions, often when the rest of the pool is at its worst.

The **corner** of the pool is the last feeding station to consider, and it's a dandy. The **corner** is in strong contention with the **lip** of the pool as the "primary feeding station." If the largest fish in the pool is not on the **lip,** he is probably in the **corner**.

The **corner** is easy to fish and easy to identify, if you know what you are looking for, and take the time to identify it.

We all fall short in this last requirement, looking for it. I really get disgusted with myself when, after fishing a pool, I head on up to the next pool and almost step in a good **corner** feeding station before I see it. There is no *good* excuse for this, but the reason is understandable.

Many excellent **corner** feeding stations are tiny. Couple this with the fact that the current in them is not as impressive as that in the riffle lying close by, and it becomes apparent that one simply does not see them. This is a poor excuse, however, because it takes only a few seconds to look over the area and locate the **corner.**

The **corner** is usually located to the side of the main riffle, or shoot, entering a pool. It will be the furthest upstream piece of water you can see. Somewhat like the **back eddy** feeding station, it is formed by a current going in the opposite direction to the main flow; being pulled by the strong current in the riffle.

Your signal to move in closer, in suspicion of a good **corner** feeding station, is often a larger boulder or ledge *immediately* beside an incoming riffle. This large boulder produces an upstream dam, stopping the backwater flowing in that direction and deflecting it back into the pool.

The trout hold right where the slow backward current meets the heavy main current, but they will always be in the slow **corner** portion and always facing *away* from the main part of the pool.

Once this feeding station is identified the location of the trout can be anticipated with almost unbelievable accuracy. To show students the accuracy with which this determination can be made, I'll cast my fly to a target in a **corner** and count 3-2-1, at which point I strike and hook the trout. No joke, just fact!

The only catcher concerning **corner** feeding stations, besides taking the time to identify them, is the fact that they may be smaller than a dinner plate, and the water-guiding obstruction may not be a fender-size boulder, but a few softball-size stones.

It doesn't seem fair to the angler but, often, these small **corners** hold very large fish. What you are seeing in that dinner plate target is only the tip of the iceberg, which spreads greatly to the sides underwater.

Learning to accurately read the water in these Park streams is an on-going challenge. Stream levels, stream temperatures and the number of insects on the stream, all influence the trout's selection of feeding stations. And, once you have all of this figured out the trout can select different feeding stations for no apparent reason. That's fishing!

CHAPTER 4
SEEING THE TROUT

Developing the ability to see the trout on their feeding stations will enable you to catch more *large trout* than anything else you can do.

This, of course, is appealing to all fishermen. But, it can also lift trout fishing to a special level which many anglers find the most challenging and rewarding form of fishing.

The evolutionary steps through which a developing trout angler proceeds go something like this.

First he or she wants to catch a lot of trout. This is most apparent with youngsters and those just getting started.

The second level is manifested by the desire to catch large trout. Everyone has, at least, one foot in this water. It seems to be most important to the boaster, but then, who doesn't enjoy talking about his fish; an unfortunate problem occurs when this is the end goal, and stage three is never reached.

The third level is that of deep personal reward. It results from confronting and successfully mastering a specific angling challenge. A one-on-one contest, successfully concluded, between man and an especially wise trout, is the greatest reward achieved by advanced anglers. This may be a large trout, which would seem to link levels two and three. After all, the *king of the pool* did not reach that size by being stupid. However, under certain circumstances a modest size trout can play a tough game.

Being able to see the trout on a feeding station can get you into the third stage quickly.

It is important to realize throughout this chapter that I am not referring to those trout, probably already spooked from their feeding stations, that one sees lying close to the stream bottom in the deepest part of the pool. I am concerned with trout that are out to feed. And remember, earlier you saw that this could be a full-time job for the trout with good stream conditions.

The first requirement in learning to see fish is realizing it can be accomplished and making a conscious effort to achieve it.

Next comes the use of physical aids which simplify the job. Polarized (not just dark) sunglasses are a must. I personally like the lightest shades. A hat with a large brim, which is dark on the underneath side, is a big help. Subdued colored clothing will not enable you to actually see the fish better, but it will definitely enable you to get closer to them, thus allowing you to see them. Your clothing does not have to be conventional camouflage attire, but you sure don't want to wear your fire-orange hunting hat.

Jeff Murray utilizes polarized sunglasses and a cautious approach to locate a large brook trout before making his presentation.

When one is attempting to see a trout in a pool, the whole fish is seldom visible. Rather, there are certain "SIGNALS" which guide our eyes to a specific spot, prompting closer evaluation.

Some of these signals are very subtle, while others are more profound.

The most readily apparent signal which says, "fish here," is the trout's *movement.* This movement is often a result of his turning to take underwater food. (Certainly, sipping a natural fly from the surface could result in detected movement, but there you could see the rise form.) A flicker of reflected light from the trout's side is all that is needed to signal his movement.

Occasionally you will get a quick glimpse of something light colored under the water. This can result from a trout "whiting a nymph" as he opens his mouth, exposing his light inner lips, to take a natural insect.

Under some circumstances a feeding trout may relocate to another spot several feet away, during which his movement is easily seen. However, don't get faked out. Normally, if a trout moves that far, as you ease in to take a look, it means you have spooked him; no, not badly enough for him to race up through the pool as if his tail were on fire. But, you may have a tough time catching this fish.

Another "signal," although harder to detect than movement, is *color contrast.* This is the difference between the color of the trout and that of the specific background against which you are viewing him.

Color contrast may be as bold as the brilliant white edges of the brookie's fins against a dark brown stone, or it may be as subtle as the dark edge of the trout's tail against a slightly darker ledge.

More effort is required on your part to cue in on the *contrast* means of seeing a trout, but it is nonetheless effective. By carefully evaluating the makeup of the stream bottom, it is often possible to pick up something that looks out of place, and there's your trout. Yes, there have been many times when I've cast to fish-shaped stones, sometimes for embarrassingly long periods, coming away feeling like a fool—but, that's fishing.

The *contrast* game can be carried beyond the color aspect to help locate trout.

That straight edge at the end of the brookie's tail, when viewed from the side, can look out of place over a stream bottom composed of almost round stones. Likewise the tapered head may be his giveaway if he happens to be lying beside a solid ledge.

Anytime you see something that looks out of place, check a little closer. It might be a trout.

This is what I was doing one fall when I saw a dark trout-shaped figure lying in the bright sun over a light colored ledge. From my position in the tail of the pool, I questioned my judgment; this was one of those long, flat pools, and what I was looking at was way up in the head of the pool.

Easing myself into a better viewing position, I realized I was both right and wrong.

Sure enough, the trout was there, but what I had seen was not the trout. I had actually seen his *shadow* on the stream bottom. Even realizing I was looking at the trout's shadow, it was very difficult to refocus my eyes a few feet above that in order to pick up the trout. Only the movement of his fins said, "Here I am."

I was so impressed with this setup that I raised my camera, zoomed the lens out, and made a number of pictures to use in my schools.

I had been using fish *shadows* to locate them in spring creeks for many years, but usually these fish can be clearly seen once the shadow pulls your glance to the correct area. This was not the case with my brookie. The dorsal

41

portion of his body was so close in coloration to that of the stream bottom, I would not have seen him on a cloudy day without a shadow present.

The trout's *shadow* can be one of the best signals you have in locating the trout's position. Naturally, the sun must be out, and even then you may have to rely on seeing only a portion of the trout's shadow. Only part of his body may be in the sun, or a portion of the stream bottom over which he is lying may be so dark there is no resulting shadow.

Knowing the "signals" to look for is very important, but so is understanding the physical parameters under which you try to use them.

The position of the sun, the texture of the stream's surface and the physical make up of the stream's banks, all will govern your ability to see the trout.

Since we are compelled to fish these streams upstream in order to prevent spooking the trout, you can do little about the angle at which the sun strikes the stream in relation to your positions.

Ideally, I like the sun high and over my back. (Don't worry about your own shadow; you'll learn quickly to compensate for that.) When the sun is in this position, it is easy to see the trout. Additionally, I find I can get much closer to

William Downey drifts a dry fly over a brook trout he can clearly see. Being able to see the fish "lifts trout fishing to a special level which many anglers find the most challenging and rewarding form of angling."

the trout under these circumstances unless I present a bold silhouette. It seems almost as if the bright sun blinds them in this set up. I know that when the situation is reversed—the fish is between me and the sun—it is just like putting a spotlight on me as far as the fish is concerned; he's gone in a flash—make that a splash.

Okay, you can't move the sun, and you want to fish upstream. But, you can jockey around a little, from one side of the stream to the other as you approach a specific pool.

Take the time to evaluate the upcoming pool, glancing over it for the best feeding stations; then, considering the suns position, move in for a closer look.

The makeup of the stream's surface definitely influences your ability to see the fish.

Heavy water, below a riffle, can be difficult to penetrate, but don't hesitate to try. Often, even though it looks like a complete series of tiny white tops from the distance, you will find several little windows of flat water through which to peer. You've got it made concerning the wariness of these trout; they will often let you move very close, where you can see them, and drop a fly right on target.

A slightly choppy stream surface, created by either the wind or the current, can present a bad situation.

The problem here results from the many surfaces of reflected light, seemingly bouncing about the pool. Try to lineup this area against a dark uniform background on the far bank. A nice, big, flat boulder or ledge is perfect, and if you can use this object to help block out the incoming sun rays, so much the better. Since this problem is at its worst when the sun is on the far side of the pool you can often make this shading tactic work.

It can be amusing to watch a knowledgeable angler attempting to block the incoming sun in this manner. He will be bobbing up and down from the waist, while weaving as far from side to side as he can, without moving his feet. An untutored observer might mistake this for a ritualistic ostrich mating dance.

A surefire way to overcome a choppy surface is to carefully check the back eddies and protected areas beside boulders. This may sound like a cop out, but both of these areas hold good trout, which are best fished to once located.

Now that you know how to see the trout in the streams, a look at a few situations in which this is extremely helpful is in order.

Extremely high streams in the spring can render most feeding stations useless. The trout simply cannot hold on them. Under these circumstances many of them move into the back eddies. These large areas are difficult to fish if the trout cannot be seen. Invariably you will either drop your fly on the wrong spot, and drag will set in before it reaches the trout, or, worse, you'll hit him on the head. Then you'll see him as he runs for cover, then you'll say a few choice words about his ancestry, then you'll go on up to the next pool promising yourself you will never fish another back eddy until you can *see* the fish.

During the peak of a hatch, with ideal water levels, it is not at all unusual to find several fish rising in close proximity. Seeing the individual fish will let you cue in on the largest one while passing up the dink.

When water levels get quite low in late summer many of the feeding stations don't exist, and the wise old trout select theirs with a degree of proficiency beyond our level of comprehension.

Several areas within a pool will appear, to you, to be equal, but the trout will invariably have a preference. Here, the best game is to actually see the trout before you make your cast.

Fall, with its accompanying cooler water temperature and low streams, often finds the fish out cruising about in search of food. Now, the *only* game is to see the trout before making your presentation.

The tactic of seeing the trout definitely works; it will help you under a broad variety of circumstances. And, if you stick with this angling game long enough, it will probably become your favorite way to fish.

CHAPTER 5

TACTICS FOR MOUNTAIN TROUT

In order to successfully fish small mountain streams one must constantly adapt his tactics to the ever-changing stream conditions.

Since these conditions are altered by the natural progression of the seasons, this is the way I would like to discuss them. I'll cover the spring season (mid March through May), the summer season (June through August), and end with the fall season (September until cold weather catches you).

SPRING SEASON

Early season angling in the Park may require some experimentation in order to take the trout.

The fellows who insist, "If I can't take them on dry flies, I don't want them," may have a tough time if they stand by this code. There is absolutely nothing wrong with trying drys at this time; most of us do, and sometimes it works. If, however, the water temperature is in the thirties or if the water is really high, it might be best to switch to nymphs or streamers.

Nymph Fishing

Nymphing for trout can be extremely effective; however, in many cases it fails to be for several, rather unfortunate, reasons.

Some anglers go to nymphs *only* when dry flies fail to produce. Obviously this means tough fishing conditions, maybe so bad, in fact, that you should be taking the family for a ride on the Skyline Drive, rather than nagging the trout in the hollows.

Expecting the nymphs to produce under some of these conditions can be more of a dream than an honest, hoped for reality.

Many anglers, using nymphs only as a *substitute*, don't catch the numbers of fish on them which they feel they should, thus spawning a lack of faith, both in

45

"In order to successfully fish small mountain streams one must constantly adapt his tactics to the ever-changing stream conditions."

the fly patterns, and their abilities to use them. Nymphing tactics are different (not damning), and trying to learn them under adverse stream conditions is not being fair to yourself.

The ideal time to brush up on your nymphing tactics is later in the season, when conditions are ideal. For example, on some nice, warm, late spring day, after you've caught enough trout on drys to adequately pump up your ego, try the nymphs. Success here will give you the confidence you need to fish them under adverse conditions. Failure will show you that you need to polish your tactics.

An important aspect of early season nymph fishing is getting your imitations close to the stream bottom. Once this level is reached the drift must be under your control to facilitate strike detection.

Success in accomplishing both of these tasks will be governed, primarily, by your ability to read the water. As mentioned in Chapter 3, this is *really* the demanding part of nymph fishing.

The determination of the trout's anticipated holding positions is fairly straight forward, and the ability to identify these correctly will come quickly with experience.

Selecting the *exact* spot to drop the nymph, in order for it to drift naturally to the waiting trout, is a little more complicated. The underwater currents must be judged even though they cannot be seen. Those through which the actual nymph will drift are of primary importance, but the currents, both underwater and on the surface, come into play through their influences upon the leader and line.

Although it is seldom mentioned, your **casting position** alone will govern your ability to put all of this together.

That's right, neither your expensive rod, nor your beautiful English reel, not even your clean vest will prompt the trout to take your nymph if you select a casting position which deprives you of control. Even if the trout takes your nymph, you probably will not know it.

Control is what nymph fishing is all about: control of the fly placement, control of the drift, control of strike detection, and control in setting the hook.

This control is achieved by selecting a casting position close enough to the target and to the anticipated feeding station to put it all together. One quick giveaway that an angler is an accomplished nymph fisherman is the short line he fishes. Glenn Morrison is one of the most proficient nymph fishermen I

Gerald Racey wisely selected a casting position which permits him to be in complete control of his nymph as it drifts along the edge of the heavy water.

know, and he always fishes nymphs on a short line. If there is a trout in the stream that doesn't want to get caught, he had better keep his mouth shut when Glenn fishes his pool with nymphs.

There is always a trade-off in selecting this casting position. Realizing the importance of getting close to the trout for control can result in *crowding* him. This will definitely spook him. If he is holding close to heavy water or very deep in the pool, you may not see him run. In fact, in the latter case, he may just snuggle down a little closer to the bottom for security.

This bottom-hugger is the one a novice angler will waste a lot of time with if he sees him, not realizing he is spooked; better that he wouldn't have seen the trout at all.

Trout can often be spooked to a point that they will not run for cover, but still will not take your fly. This usually relates to how safe they, apparently, feel where they are holding. But, maybe he just isn't ready to leave yet; take one more step and he'll vanish.

Okay, you now know where you want to run your nymph, where to cast it, and where to stand. Next you must get it down to the trout's level.

Depth is no great problem. Experimenting with various weighted nymphs and several size split shot, will reveal the proper combination needed. The line control to aid in getting the nymph to the bottom can be a little tricky, with each pool presenting its own demands. Simply stated, *you must hold as much line as possible away from any currents which will pull the leader and nymph up from the bottom.* If you can do this, you'll get your nymph down to the trout. You'll notice that I did not say, "Catch the trout." At this stage you're only halfway home in nymph fishing; the easy half.

The most difficult part of nymph fishing in small mountain streams is detecting the strike.

Casting upstream, it is desirable to have the nymph drift back down in a natural manner, unimpeded by the leader. This is the way the naturals act, and the trout are accustomed to seeing this. They readily take the artificial nymphs drifting in this manner. However, they don't make a big deal of it; no fanfare, no fireworks, and, unfortunately, seldom a twitch in the leader.

A comment I often hear in my schools is, "Oh, I felt the strike, but I missed him." That's exactly right. If you are unaware that a trout has picked up your nymph until you feel him, you will miss the majority of your strikes. You should *see* your strikes.

Realizing that you have only a second to a second and a half between the time the trout picks up your nymph and the time he ejects it, as a phony, tells you that not only must you instantly detect his take, but also that you strike him quickly.

This is where the fluorescent butt leaders and the indicators discussed in Chapter 2 come into play.

There are many devices which can be attached to the leader to aid in strike detection. These range from a dry fly bobbing above the upper part of the leader to cork, yarn, vinyl, foam, or plastic indicators attached to the leader. Most are helpful in strike detection, but some cast like the Goodyear Blimp would attached to a 4X tippet. Some float a little too well, robbing you of the necessary depth required in nymphing.

The Scientific Anglers indicators offer, what I consider, the best compromise. They are highly visible, do not impede the nymph's action, and cast smoothly. Several can be used on one leader if needed, placing the first one, three feet above the nymph and another a foot or so above the first one.

When fishing I watch these closely. A slight hesitation or change of direction of the indicator as the nymph drifts downstream is my cue to strike the trout. If I cannot see the indicators, I watch the bright butt section of the leader in order to detect a trout picking up the nymph.

Once a take is noted it is impossible to strike the trout too quickly; too hard, yes, but not too quickly.

The basic nymphing method for mountain trout streams is the **dead drift** technique where the nymph is cast upstream and allowed to drift downstream in a natural manner. This, hopefully, simulates the action of a natural nymph being carried by the current.

Using fairly short casts, the nymph is delivered up or up and across stream at a very slight angle, and no action is imparted to the fly as it drifts back downstream.

The **Leisenring lift** is a similar technique except as the fly reaches the anticipated feeding station the rod tip is gently lifted higher, bringing the nymph up through the current in a swimming motion. Here, you are attempting to convince the trout a real nymph is emerging to the surface. This tempting getaway action will often stimulate a trout to strike which ignored a dead drifting pattern.

A third nymph fishing tactic which is effective in the Park is what I call **swing nymphing.** This is a variation of a method Charlie Brooks taught me years ago on the Madison River in Montana.

Swing nymphing is most effective in large, deep pools, which is great, since these are tough to fish with conventional dead drifting tactics.

Let's assume the spring rains have your stream quite full of water. You are standing beside a beautiful large pool, but as you check the lip, you realize there is too much water for any fish to hold there. The head of the pool looks like Niagara Falls, so you don't have a chance there. A close evaluation of the edges for back eddies and feeding corners reveals there are none in this pool. As a last resort you check the mid-pool area. Sure enough, there are several large boulders below the stream surface which could block the current to provide protected feeding stations for several trout.

Realizing these fish will be holding on the bottom and that you must get your nymph down through four feet of *fast water* (unfortunately, this is no mill pond) presents a problem.

Conventional dead drifts, where the line is retrieved at the same rate as the drifting nymph, are out since you can't wade up far enough through the deep tail. Even if you could force your way in from below, the fast current would quickly drag your line and leader, pulling the nymph up from the bottom.

Enter **swing nymphing.** Standing ten to fifteen feet to the side of the underwater boulders and almost even with them, you cast your weighted nymph fifteen feet upstream, carefully dropping it into the same current which is flowing to the boulders.

At the next step, the swing nymphing begins to differ greatly from the dead drifting approach.

Rather than retrieving any extra slack line with the line hand, the nymph is allowed to sink on a loose leader. Only after the nymph has reached its maximum depth and is drifting toward the anticipated feeding station, is any line recovered with the line hand.

Simultaneously with this gradual stripping action, the rod is extended out over the stream as far as you can reach and up in the air at about a forty-five degree angle.

At this point the actual fishing of the nymph begins. While maintaining a tight line from the line hand all the way to the nymph, the rod is used to guide the nymph into the desired location. As the current pushes the nymph downstream, the whole arm is swung in a wide arc at the same rate the nymph is moving. This enables you to hold the line and leader away from any currents which would interfere with the deep drift of the nymph.

With this technique it is often possible to *feel* the strike; however, it is usually very subtle. You must be constantly alert in order to detect this strike in time to set the hook.

Even with the potential for feeling this strike, it is wise to watch your indicators and the fluorescent butt section of your leader closely.

Not only do they help in strike detection with this technique, but they are your greatest aids in letting you know if your nymph is reaching the desired depth. Seeing your lowest indicator drifting only inches below the stream's surface tells you that your nymph is not getting close enough to the bottom. This means that either you are not adequately reaching across the fast currents, which are pulling your leader and nymph up from the stream bottom, or that you cast too far across the current to start with. As before, the whole nymphing game depends upon line control.

Streamer Fishing

The spring season is the best time for streamer fishing. Full streams and discolored waters are your signals to reach for these minnow imitations.

Conventional streamer tactics of casting across or down and across stream and stripping the fly back are not very productive in these mountain streams. More finesse is required if one expects a reasonable degree of success.

A major problem with wading and fishing downstream in these small streams is that you will scare many of the trout with your approach. Since these fish are facing into the current, they can easily see you as you move into casting position. For this reason, your best hope is to take them off the far side of the pool and from the middle of the deep pools.

This is fine in theory, but getting the streamer to the bottom at this angle can be difficult. As soon as it touches the water, the strong current between you and the fly can grab the leader and rip the fly out of the desired area. Hopes that maybe a trout lying further down in the pool will take the streamer are seldom rewarded since it is usually swinging only inches below the surface at this point.

Your best chance to take a trout with the basic down and across presentation will occur by carefully fishing the back eddies on the far side of the stream. Slow currents here will permit the streamer to reach the bottom, and if you can keep some heavy water between the trout and yourself, the trout may not get spooked.

Picking the pockets with a downstream approach can be a successful streamer tactic in full streams. Let's assume there are several bushel-basket size boulders lying a foot or two apart in the lower portion of a pool. The water here is about three feet deep and moving at a good pace.

The trout will be holding close to the stream bottom around these boulders and thus should not be easily scared as you approach from upstream. The main problem here, is that they will seldom pull up very far off the bottom to take a fly, and getting the streamer down to them might be difficult.

Your best drifts will come by carefully evaluating the currents approaching these boulders and placing your streamer so that these will carry it to the trout. Once this is achieved you should slowly swim the fly through the hot spot. You do not want a rapid stripping action here which is often associated with streamer fishing. Rather, you want to make your offering look like a real minnow swept into these pockets by the current. Watch your leader and indicator carefully to be sure you have a tight line all the way down to the fly. The mixed currents can produce a momentarily slack leader, and if the trout picks up your fly at this instant you will not know it. Yes, you have to set the hook; your leader will not be tight enough for the trout to hook himself.

A slight variation of the swinging nymph technique is effective when fishing streamers in the deep mid-pool areas. Here you are wading downstream, casting upstream, and fishing the water beside and slightly below you.

Gerald Racey uses the **bounce retrieve** *method of fishing a streamer in the Park. "This basic upstream style streamer fishing is the most successful method . . . to fish streamers in small mountian streams."*

Fortunately, this is not as difficult as it sounds. For example, you have just waded down along the side of a large pool with a deep mid-pool area. After evaluating the speed of the current and the depth of the water, you realize casting your streamer down or across stream would fail to get it anywhere close to the stream bottom.

Positioning yourself even with or slightly above the deepest part of the pool, you cast your streamer ten to fifteen feet up and across stream. A well weighted streamer and a split shot on the leader will help in gaining adequate depth, but you still must handle the line properly to prevent the negative influences of the heavy current.

Allow the streamer to sink on a slack leader, and refrain from stripping any line or leader until it reaches the deep part of the pool. At this point the rod is extended out and up at about a forty-five degree angle above the stream. The slack line and leader are now retrieved with the line hand until you think you are tight to the streamer but not lifting it. The indicators will help you know when the proper amount of line is retrieved. If you can't see an indicator five feet above the fly you know you haven't stripped in enough line; if the indicator is several feet out of the water you know you've overdone it. Remember, the Scientific Anglers indicators are visible several feet below the stream's surface at these short ranges, so take advantage of this in getting your streamer where it should be.

At this point, the manner of fishing the streamer differs from that of the swinging nymph.

Since the minnows are capable of more movement along the stream bottom than most of the Park's nymphs, it is desirable to impart a slight darting action to the streamer. In addition to mimicking the minnow's action, this assures you of keeping a tight line on the streamer, which is a great help in detecting the trout's strike. I prefer to use the line-hand to impart this darting-action to the streamer while using the rod to guide the drift.

One word of caution concerning this technique. If you overdo the darting action or fail to bridge the fast currents with your extended fly rod, you may pull the fly far enough up off the stream bottom that the trout will not come up after it.

A variation of this technique, which I use when fishing a streamer straight upstream or up and across stream at a slight angle, is the **bounce retrieve.**

This is different from the first two methods of streamer fishing in that I wade upstream as well as cast upstream.

Upon delivery, the streamer is permitted to sink and start its drift back downstream. The line-hand is used to retrieve the slack line, assuring continuous contact with the streamer, once adequate depth is achieved. As the fly rides naturally along the stream bottom, the rod is lifted about a foot and then dropped to its original position every several feet of the drift. This bouncing action often motivates trout to strike that were not attracted to a dead drift.

This basic upstream style of streamer fishing is the most successful method I have found to fish streamers in small mountain streams. Many slight variations of fly play can be used as long as you maintain a tight line on the streamer in order to detect the strike.

Dry Fly Fishing

Dry flies can definitely be effective during the spring season in the Park. Even if you do not mop up with them on your first trip of the season, while there is snow on the ground, rest assured the streams will warm quickly, and they will soon come into their own.

Many dry fly possibilities face William Downey as he works his way upstream. "Accurate fly placement and a natural drift are both very important..." when fishing these mini-pools in the spring.

Two natural factors beyond your control have great influences upon the trout's willingness to feed upon the surface; the temperature of the water and the volume of the water in the stream.

For example, if the water temperature is forty-two degrees and the streams are quite low, I would expect to catch trout on drys. But, I have had many days in these mountains when the water temperature was in the mid-forties and the streams were high when the trout wouldn't look up.

Reflecting upon the trout's natural characteristics, covered in Chapter 3, will explain this and help you determine when and where to fish drys at this time of the year.

Because the trout is cold-blooded, his metabolic need for food increases as the water temperature increases (up to a certain point). But the feeding must be done in an efficient manner in order for the food to help the trout live and grow. From a biological point, this means the food must provide more sustenance than the energy required to capture it.

Don't break out your book on ichthyology; to the angler this means the trout *must* capture the maximum amount of food with the least amount of effort.

Incorporating this logic into dry dry fishing means you must concentrate on specific feeding stations that supply a reasonable amount of food, yet do not have a really fast current.

As you approach a pool from below, take a few minutes to evaluate the *whole pool;* plan your strategy for fishing each worthy feeding station. Then, work your way through the pool in a manner that will enable you to fish each area without spooking the trout on the next feeding station.

Selecting the proper type dry fly for early season conditions is important. It should be an exceptionally good floater (which the high water will thoroughly test) and be easy for you to see on the choppy surface. The Royal Wulff and Dark Goofus in sizes 12 and 14 have always been good early season patterns, but they really don't match the natural insects very well.

The first significant hatch to occur is the Quill Gordon (Epeorus pleuralis). The artificial Quill Gordon dry fly has long been the standard for this hatch, but I find it difficult to keep this delicate pattern floating on rough water. The Mr. Rapidan dry fly developed fifteen years ago to match this first insect, while providing excellent angler visibility and floating qualities, has become the favorite fly for many early season anglers. The thinking is that if there is no hatch the trout may readily take the Royal Wulff, but if the trout have become accustomed to sipping, even a few, natural Quill Gordon mayflies, why take a chance; give them a Mr. Rapidan dry in a size 12 or 14.

Accurate fly placement and a natural drift are both very important so don't go to a real find leader tippet. A 7½ to 9 foot leader tapered to 4X will be just about right for this size fly with typical early spring conditions.

Okay, back to the stream. You've checked the whole pool for potential surface feeding areas. The **corners** and **back eddies** have always been good early in the season, and this pool appears to have both. However, the **lip** is right there in front of you so give it a try.

55

You must stay far enough below it to prevent scaring a trout holding on it and yet close enough to bridge the fast current dropping over the lip with your rod. You want to hold all of the line and most of the leader, out of the water.

Cast your dry about four-feet up into the pool, carefully dropping it in the precise current which will deliver it to the feeding station. If you did not scare him and if you do not get drag, the trout will rise to your fly, if he's there. The *only* reason for a trout to be in this part of the pool is to feed. If you play the game properly you'll catch him on the first drift.

The **tail** and **mid-pool** feeding stations seldom provide good dry fly fishing early in the spring. The customary lack of protected feeding areas here usually prompts any hungry trout to locate elsewhere.

The **back eddy** is such a place. The gentle currents here are the main attraction for the trout early in the spring. Little effort is required from the trout to hold in these areas, and when something good to eat comes along he can easily capture it.

The **corner** feeding station appeals to the trout when the streams are very high for much the same reasons as the back eddy. The rate of the current will probably be greater in the **corner** than in the **back eddy**, but it is usually nullified by the boulder which creates it.

The trout holding on a **corner** feeding station is the easiest fish in the pool to catch. You got lucky on this—he's also probably the largest trout in the pool. Yes, the combination of protection for the fish and the easy access to any food funneled to the area cause the **corner** to be the primary dry fly feeding station when the streams are full.

To fish the corners, I like to approach them from the far side of the stream, using the heavy water in the riffle to conceal my wading. It is normally possible to get within eight to ten feet of the corner in this manner. Casting a dry fly to the far side of the corner permits the current to drift it right to the waiting trout. It is *extremely important* to hold all of the line out of the water as the fly drifts to the trout. In many cases if you have more than six inches—that's right six inches—of leader on the water, you will get drag before your fly reaches the trout, and you just botched your best chance to take the largest and easiest trout in the pool.

* * * * *

Making a second trip to the Park, this time in mid-April, you find the streams much lower than they were earlier. They are not too low, but rather, just right. There are many feeding stations available to the trout in each pool, and the stream is still full enough to help hide your approach.

The Quill Gordons are still on, in fact, there are more of them on the water than before. The Blue Quills appear to be at their peak, and the March Browns are starting to emerge.

Charley Waterman of Montana cautiously fishes a dry fly to the Park's brookies. Even in the spring, it is often best to approach these trout on your hands and knees.

As you approach the first pool from below, there is a trout rising on the lip. In your excitement, you miss the target with your dry fly, but as it drifts toward the lip the trout swims two feet further than you thought he would and sips in your fly.

There are so many flies on the water the trout's normally cautious concern about exposing himself is overridden by his desire to feed. Having encountered conditions like this previously, you assume you are in for some great fishing. Oh, you can't step on the trout's tail and expect to catch him, and it would be better if you did not accidently fall down in the same pool you are trying to fish, but all things being equal you should have great fishing.

Noting some disturbance among the grapefruit size stones to the side of the main current in mid-pool, you move in for a closer look. No rise form, but again you see something moving close to the bank where the water is only six inches deep. Now you see him; sure enough, it's a large trout feeding underwater. Having encountered this in previous years, you realize the game he's playing.

The March Brown nymphs move to these areas from their previous homes in deep water just prior to emerging. The concentration of these large nymphs prompts the trout to move in and feed upon them.

The first drift of your dry fly takes this trout. As you are carefully releasing him, you notice another fish feeding in the same area only a short distance above where the first one was. Confidently, you cast your dry fly to this fish, but much to your surprise, he does not take it. Four successive casts fail to interest him, even though you can clearly see he is actively feeding on natural insects.

Preferring to assume this trout has a one track mind, and not that he is smarter than you are, you replace your dry fly with a size 12 March Brown nymph. Moving slightly to the far side of the stream, so your leader will not drift over the trout before the nymph, you make your pitch. Yep, that's what he wanted! Even though these brookies are seldom selective in their feeding, it can happen when there is an abundance of one specific insect.

Throughout the next two hours the trout take your dry flies quite well in all parts of the pools. The fishing is almost too easy—almost.

Later the air temperature drops, and the adult mayfly duns don't make the fast getaway from the stream surface they did earlier. This is great because it presents them as easy targets to the trout longer. It isn't until you start fishing for a specific trout you find feeding in the back eddy that you realize some of the trout have changed their manner of feeding.

This trout is rising to take a natural fly about every fifteen to twenty seconds; however, he won't take your size 14 March Brown dry fly—the same one his neighbors had found so appealing all day. Knowing the Little Blue Quills are also hatching, you taper your leader down to 6X and drift a size 16 Blue Quill dry fly over him—nothing. To make you feel even more dejected, he almost swamps your fly on the third drift as he rises to take a natural only two inches from your fly.

Having caught a fair number of fish this day, you decide to stick with this fish and see just what's going on. Moving in as close to the feeding trout as you assume he will permit, you get down close to the water's surface to see just what he is taking. There are a fair number of Blue Quill Duns riding the surface, but the trout isn't taking them. You can now see the fish clearly, and he doesn't budge when a dun drifts by. Finally, you can see what he is feeding on—the emerging Blue Quills. The cool air temperature has slowed the rate at which the flies rid themselves of the nymph case to pop their wings, and the trout is taking them as they struggle in the surface film.

Very seldom are these brookies this selective, but it can happen. Attaching a size 16 Blue Quill numph to the 5X tippet of your leader, you dress the whole leader with silicon cream right down to the nymph and even work a small amount into the nymph's wing pad.

You intentionally throw a little extra slack into the leader as you cast the nymph a foot above the trout. Holding your breath, you carefully watch the nymph drift closer to the trout. He rises and sucks in your nymph, just as he had all those naturals. He was certainly a tough trout to outsmart, but then those are the best teachers.

Streamers are not really necessary since the water level has dropped, but they can be used as a change-of-pace fly. Some of the large, deep pools would be the best places to fish them. The clarity of the water and the reduced volume would enable the trout to see you if you approach them from above, therefore, the best tactic is the bounce retrieve presented upstream.

One motivation for using streamers in the lower water level, would be to brush up on your underwater technique. If you are not completely confident in your ability to fish nymphs upstream dead drift, cheat a little and practice with a size 10 Woolly Bugger. Casting up or up and across stream, let the fly sink to the bottom; retrieve all the slack until you are sure you are tight to the fly. Fish the streamer back downstream using the bounce retrieve described earlier, never allowing any slack to develop in the leader. This tight line will simplify strike detection, enabling you to catch a fair number of trout which will build confidence in fishing underwater.

Spin Fishing

The first two months of the season are the best times to fish in the Park with spinning tackle. The full streams give you more room to work your spoons and spinners, and the fish are not as skittish as they will be later in the season.

There are two basic techniques which are effective with spinning tackle in these small streams. Although the manner of fishing and lure-play differ greatly, these methods are dictated primarily by the direction the fishermen choose to fish.

The downstream approach is the most popular. Here the fisherman cautiously approaches the heads of the pools from the sides. If the pool is large enough, the first cast can be made across stream, and the lure is retrieved across the current until it reaches a slight angle below the fisherman, where it must be cranked back against the current.

The next cast would be made across, and slightly downstream, and retrieved in the same manner as the first cast. This pattern can be continued with each cast reaching a little further downstream until the whole pool is covered.

Varying the speed of the retrieve and mixing in some darting action, applied with the rod tip, will enable you to find the most effective tactics for the existing water conditions.

Small Rapalas and size 0 Mepps are two of the most popular lures to use with this approach. Since both of these come with treble hooks when purchased, you must either replace them with a single hook or use pliers to cut off all but one hook in order to comply with the Park's regulations. Remember, also, that on the fish-for-fun streams you are required to fish with *barbless* hooks, so you must mash down the hook's barb or file it off, or both, in order to obtain a smooth hook.

The second method of fishing with spinning tackle in these head-water streams is to work your way upstream. Here you would move into the lower part of each pool and cast your lure up or up and across stream.

It is possible to get your lures deeper with this approach, and you have a little more leeway in lure-play.

Small spoons, such as 1/32 or 1/16 oz. Eppinger Daredevil, are very effective when fished upstream. Rather than crank them back at a uniform rate, a slow jigging action is often best.

Small jigs can also be good fished upstream with a jigging action. The game is to allow the lure to sink to the stream bottom; then, every several feet of the drift, slowly lift and drop the rod tip in order to bounce the lure along the bottom.

SUMMER SEASON

Summer brings lower streams, a reduction in the variety of aquatic insects, and more demanding conditions. But, it also brings the type trout fishing serious anglers consider to be the most challenging.

Summer conditions produce "skittish trout" prompting William Downey to make a long cast. This is an ideal time to use a 2-weight rod.

Every pool will have several fish on feeding stations, but they can be very difficult to catch. This is definitely a time to "duplicate what nature is doing."

The only mayfly left for the trout, which is present in large numbers, is the Sulphur. Charlie Foxes' Sulphur Spinner in sizes 16 and 18 is the most successful fly pattern I've found to match this hatch in the Park.

Unfortunately, selecting the proper fly is only a small part of summer trout fishing. Before approaching a pool closely, I always study it carefully to see if I can locate a fish or two on feeding stations. Sometimes they will giveaway their presence by rising to take a natural fly from the surface, but other times it is necessary to search the water until the trout can be seen.

Once the trout is located, it is very important to select the proper casting position, and even more important to choose the correct avenue of approach. The trout are now very skittish so in some cases it is even necessary to crawl into casting position. Once I'm in position I like to wait a few minutes before making a cast. If the trout is feeding, I wait for him to take three insects. If the natural food is sparse I wait about two minutes. This pause does two things; it gives the trout time to reassure himself that all is normal, in case I made a little disturbance moving in, and it lets me steady my nerves. Yes, I still get excited when I see a feeding trout.

Accurate fly placement is very important, but I do not like to "measure my cast" by false casting over the trout. This is an excellent method for determining the precise amount of line needed to reach a trout when the water levels are higher, but it is almost a surefire way to spook him now.

If it is necessary to lengthen the line in order to reach the trout it is better to do it by false casting to the side, well below his position. Then turn and make the presentation in one smooth forward motion.

The fly and leader must land on the water very lightly or they will scare the trout. I like to use a 9-foot leader tapered to 6X to help get a delicate presentation. This fine tippet also enables the fly to drift naturally to the trout. In most cases, the trout will rise and sip in your offering on the first drift, if you have done everything right. Remember, he is there to feed, and with the scarcity of food, he must feed on everything he can. Turning to take a natural insect, which would prevent him from seeing your fly, is the only natural reason he would not rise to your pattern. If he sees your fly and does not take it on the first drift it is highly unlikely he will take it at all.

At this point you have two choices. You can admit the trout is smarter than you are, give up on him, and go find another one, or, you can hang in there and try to outsmart him. The first option can be humiliating, but the second one can waste a lot of time, and there is a good chance you still won't take him, which really makes you feel inadequate.

However, I have a hard time walking away from a feeding trout. These one-on-one contests are just too challenging. No longer is there a question of where the trout is located; you can clearly see him. Nor is there any question as to whether or not he is in the mood to feed; he's gobbling everything that comes within reach—except your fly. The ground rules are right down to the nitty-gritty; it's you against the trout.

The route I take usually goes something like this. If he refuses my fly on the first drift I'll put it back over him two more times, but no more. Continually pounding a trout with the same fly usually puts him down. If, as in a situation like this, I know a specific fly is hatching, even sparsely, I'll use another hatch matcher. In this case a size 18 Grey Yellow No Hackle Dun would be a logical choice. If this does not take him, I go to a much smaller fly with an entirely different silhouette. This fly is not selected by chance, but rather, it is carefully chosen to match another type food which the trout is accustomed to seeing at this time of the year. Black ants are numerous during the summer months so this is a logical choice. I definitely want the trout to see the new fly, but not too well; the larger the fly, the easier it is for them to realize it's not the real thing. In order to play it safe, while still having good hooking qualities, I'll choose a size 20 Black Ant.

I'll give the trout time to feed for a few more minutes; some fish develop a feeding rhythm, and my chances of taking him are best if I drift my fly over him in this sequence.

I am going to be very careful with this presentation; I want the first drift to be perfect. This means I must drop the fly very delicately on the water—if the leader slaps the water, I've had it. The cast must be angled correctly so that the leader does not drift over the trout before the fly gets to him.

One of the most frustrating things which can happen is to successfully accomplish these first two steps; then, as the trout rises to take the fly, drag sets in causing him to refuse it at the last second. The best way to prevent this is either to throw a little slack in the leader or to drop the fly only a short distance above the trout on carefully selected currents.

In most cases this fish will take an Ant. If, however, it is refused you can try a few more small flies or rest the trout and come back later to try him.

July and August usually present the most demanding fishing of the season. Low water conditions, sparse hatches and spooky fish are now the norm. Sure, you can still catch fish, but there won't be any freebies.

There are some small Olive Caddisflies and Little Yellow Stoneflies on the water, and the trout take them readily. However, terrestrial insects now comprise the major portion of the trout's diet.

Fly patterns imitating ants, beetles, crickets, and grasshoppers are very effective in the Park in late summer. Size 16 is the maximum, 18 is better, and often it is necessary to go smaller.

I prefer to use 9 foot leaders tapered to 6X at this time of the year and to fish them on the most delicate rods I can find.

I now use a two-weight outfit for all my summer and fall mountain trout fishing. There is no doubt in my mind that the improved fishing I've had during low water conditions in recent years is directly attributable to these rods. The delicate and accurate presentations possible with a good two-weight outfit are almost unbelievable.

Some time ago I did extensive testing with seven different two-weight rods. All of these rods were pretty good in these small mountain streams. However, some needed to be over-lined to load properly, which was not desirable for the most delicate presentations. Some lacked accuracy on the longest casts, while performing well in close.

I felt one particular 8 foot model was well ahead of the others. In fact, I went ahead and had a second tip built for the rod as a little extra insurance.

* * * * *

A size 16 Shenk's Cricket is an excellent summer pattern in the Park; it passes for many natural trout foods.

During low rainfall years some of the Park's streams get very low. Some stretches of certain streams even go dry. When this condition gets bad the Park officials wisely close the streams most drastically affected, and have, under extreme situations, closed all of the streams to fishing.

63

Even prior to the official closing of specific streams, many conscientious anglers stop fishing the lowest streams. The reduced stream flows, lower water oxygen content, and higher water temperatures adversely stress the trout. However they have a tremendous capacity to rebound from these conditions— I have seen them do just this dozens of times.

The worst problem for the brookies, when there is a greatly reduced stream flow, is the water snake. When many trout are locked into a few isolated pools there is not enough cover for all of them, and the snakes take a great toll. This is the time for anglers to leave the trout alone, even on a voluntary basis, if not so regulated. What happens is, the trout flee from the angler only to swim into an exposed position below a waiting snake—zap.

FALL SEASON

From September until the Park's fishing season closes on October 15, the fishing is better than it was late in the summer. (The fish-for-fun streams are open year-round.)

During September "the cool nights . . . along with nature's clock, telling them to get ready for the rapidly approaching spawning season, sparks the trout's desire to feed."

There are often September rains which improve the water levels. Even if these do not materialize, the cool nights drop the water temperatures to more comfortable levels for the trout. This, along with nature's clock telling them to get ready for the rapidly approaching spawning season, sparks their desire to feed.

In addition to the same varieties of terrestrial insects present all summer, the Chironomidae Midges start appearing on the streams in September.

A typical condition one would expect to find on these streams in mid-September would be something like this.

Careful evaluation of an average pool would reveal a small fish or two holding on feeding stations in the lower portion. You could fish for these trout, and you would probably land one of them. However, the commotion this would make could scare his roommate, causing him to dart up through the pool, killing your chances for another trout in the pool.

If you can withstand the temptation of these small fish and look beyond them to carefully study the rest of the pool, you will probably locate a big fish or two. However, at this point, only experience will tell you these are the kings of the pool.

You will see a very delicate rise form, then another, and then another. Most likely, these will occur on the side of the main part of the pool in a back eddy. The water is so low now, it is impossible to tell if there is any current in the back eddy. If so, which direction is it flowing where the rises occurred?

You must move in close enough to actually see the trout in order to know where to cast your fly. Finally, after sneaking to within fifteen feet of the closest rise form, you spot him. And, he's a dandy!

The cool water temperature has put him in the mood to feed, and the abundance of terrestrial insects and midges on the surface are just what he wants. Unfortunately there is not enough current to bring this food to the trout as fast as he wants it, so he *cruises* just below the stream's surface, sipping in all the insects which come within view.

Remain motionless, and let him take a few more naturals in order to determine his cruising pattern. Whatever you do, don't make a move when he is headed toward you. This would quickly scare him, chasing him under a boulder and ending the contest. Rather, wait until he has made his turn and is headed away from you to make your cast.

Delicately drop a size 20 Black Jassid about a foot ahead of the trout and into his anticipated cruising path. If your timing is right and your fly settles gently to the stream, you have a good chance of taking this trout. The Jassid matches many of the minute insects the trout is accustomed to feeding on, so it is unlikely he will refuse to rise because of the pattern. The most common reasons for failing to catch this trout are a sloppy presentation, or having the trout turn before he gets to the fly and not see it.

If you are guilty of the former reason, just call this a learning experience, and go find another trout. If he did not see your fly, you still have a chance to take him. Wait until he is well past it; then gently retrieve it and try him again.

This is very challenging fishing, but it is extremely rewarding.

* * * * *

If fall rains bring the streams up (they always come up a little after the trees lose their leaves,) you can use the same basic tactics which were successful in late-spring. Drys, nymphs, and streamers all work, but you will probably want to use smaller flies and lighter tippets now.

Nice additions to fall angling are the leaf-jams. A little extra stream volume, after the leaves are on the water, can cause them to pile up like miniature dams in the tails of some pools. There are almost always several good fish feeding in front of these leaf-jams, and they can be very easy to catch. Standing below the leaf-jam, cast a dry fly several feet up into the pool, and let it drift naturally. The trout usually rise and sip in the fly just as it approaches the leaves.

The precise spawning time for the brook trout varies from year to year. I have seen many fish on the beds before the season closes on October 15. Most anglers feel it is unethical to fish for the trout while they are on the spawning beds. Even if

"The spawning beds are easy to identify; the slight depression of cleanly swept gravel stands out so vividly one would almost assume they are illuminated with spotlights." Note how William Downey carefully avoids the spawning area in front of him.

you plan to return all of the trout to the stream, there is a chance the stress caused by being caught can interfere with successful spawning. Why take the chance?

The spawning beds are easy to identify; the slight depressions of cleanly swept gravel stand out so vividly one would almost assume they are illuminated with spotlights. No angler would be so thoughtless as to wade through these beautiful nests of future trout. However, a few weeks after spawning has been accomplished, many of these beds lose their sheen and are difficult to identify at a glance. The angler should now take a little extra care to identify spawning areas before wading through any pool. The eggs are very susceptible to damage, and it takes only a few seconds to plot a course which would prevent wading through the beds.

Excellent angling is often possible after spawning has been completed. This may not last very long; as the water temperatures drop, so does the trout's need for food.

Late fall tactics are much like those used early in the spring. Nymphs drifted naturally along the stream bottom will probably take more trout than dry flies. The water levels are normally lower than those encountered in the spring, producing more wary trout. Thus, the angling game is much more demanding in the fall.

In summary: You will find that your best angling will result from keenly observing the many continuing changes occurring in and around the streams, and then carefully adjusting your tactics to meet these conditions.

CHAPTER 6
BACKPACKING AND TROUT FISHING

It is not necessary to pack into the backcountry and spend a night or two in order to have good trout fishing in the Park. However, backpacking and mountain trout fishing blend well together, producing a very rewarding experience.

Not being rushed to head out of the hollows before darkness falls will enable you to take advantage of the abundance of aquatic insects present at dusk.

For example, my son Jeff and I recently packed into a Park stream i had fished often over the years and felt I knew well. The stretch we were on was a long hike from the closest road, and prior to our camping trip I had never been able to fish it until dusk.—I respect rattlesnakes too much to hike very far in these mountains in the dark.

Having only about an hour to fish, after setting up the tent, we decided to fish until we could no longer see our flies on the water. There was a sparse mayfly dance over the stream, and a few spent Sulphur spinners were falling onto the surface. The first several pools all produced brookies, which were located by seeing rise forms. The later we fished the more flies fell onto the stream; more flies meant more rising fish, and soon there were feeding trout everywhere. The last pool I fished that evening was narrow and very long; the trout were in a line from the tail of the pool to the head, as if in a pre-determined tactical position to assure no spent Sulphur drifted all the way through the pool.

The fishing was outstanding because of the concentration of spent flies, and had we not been spending the night there, we would have missed it.

* * * * *

Backcountry camping will get you away from other anglers simply because of the amount of time required to reach a specific area. It also enables you to make the best use of your time.

Certain sections of some streams are so far from the closest access roads that to hike in, fish them, and then hike out the same day would mean spending more time hiking than fishing. And, if you left your car up on the Skyline Drive and are compelled to climb back up the mountain, after one of these marathon days, you may have some of the same suspicions many of us hold. Speculations among longtime Park anglers venture that some mysterious little fellow lives along the top of these mountains with the assigned purpose of raising the top of the mountains as tired anglers start their long pull back up, after fishing all day. I even thought I saw him one evening; but now as I think about it, I realize I was too tired to see straight.

Getting back away from the roads can also provide better fishing. Many serious Park anglers do not kill any of their fish, feeling that *each trout is too valuable to be caught only once.* However, some fellows still keep their trout; often the further you go into the backcountry, the more fish you find. There is one problem that can occur in this respect. Some backpackers talk romantically about how great it is to cook their freshly caught trout for the evening meal, proudly volunteering that they only kill what they plan to eat. The problem with this logic is that they fail to realize the negative impact this can have on these fragile streams if all backpacking anglers do the same thing.

* * * * *

Gerald Racey fishes a remote Park stream. "Getting back away from the roads can . . . provide better fishing."

No special fishing tackle is required for the backpacking. However, since you will be carrying less than you usually do to lighten the load, each item should be carefully selected. Take only those items which have proven to be worthy for mountain trout fishing. This is no place to test that new rod or to experiment with an unusual leader design or to test a whole boxful of untried fly patterns. You don't have to take a lot of tackle, but it had better be right, or you will have a very frustrating trip.

Small, multi-piece pack rods are nice for this type fishing, but they are not a must. You should, however, make sure the rod you use in the little streams will load properly with a number four or smaller line size. Have several extra leaders and ample tippet material. One medium size fly box will hold all the flies you need. These should be selected to cover the specific needs you expect to encounter *at the time of your trip.* If you are not familiar with the seasonal food fluctuations check the charts in Chapter 1. A properly stocked fly box for an April trip could let you down badly in early August.

Foot gear for this type hiking and fishing is a matter of personal preference. The main thing to keep in mind is that you want to have a safe footing on the trails as well as in the streams. Injuries from bad falls are much more dangerous when they occur a long way from civilization. Be sure to carry a first aid kit and a snakebite kit. A small whistle, capable of shrill blasts, is good insurance if you are alone.

Always let someone know where you will be; even if it's your family or fishing buddy back at home. If you do not show up at the appointed time, at least someone will know where to look for you.

Getting lost in the park's backcountry is a real possibility. I have gotten lost twice, and I can assure you it is a very uncomfortable feeling.

I once came across two fellows who were close to panic, as they raced up a trail begging me to tell them where they were and how to get out. These fellows were miles from where they thought they were, and the shortest route I could plot for them to get back to the Skyline Drive still caused them to be five hours late in meeting their group. This whole problem resulted from a poorly sketched map.

Anyone camping, or even just fishing, the Park's backcountry should have a good set of maps. There are three maps which completely cover the Park. These are designated as Northern, Central, and Southern Section Maps. They portray in detail streams, elevations, trails, shelters, roads, and facilities.

Maps are available from either:

Murray's Fly Shop
P.O. Box 156
Edinburg, VA 22824
(703) 984-4212

Shenandoah Natural History Association
Shenandoah National Park
Rt. 4, Box 348
Luray, VA 22835

* * * * *

The following are some of the suggestions, rules, and regulations governing backcountry camping as set forth by the Shenandoah National Park.

THINK AHEAD

When you explore the backcountry, you have to live out of your knapsack. And you face what seems a contradiction: you must take everything you need for the trip; yet, travel light. Result: You get down to life's basic necessities in a hurry.

With such choices to make, you'll find it is important to plan your wilderness journey ahead of time. Here are some things to consider:

Compass—A good azimuth compass teams up well with a topographic map to give you the land navigation tools you need.

Backpack—Join in the lively discussions all backpackers enjoy about what makes the lightest, best balanced, most easily carried packboard, knapsack and frame, or rucksack—then make your own choice.

Clothing—Choose clothing that suits Shenandoah's changeable, cool, sometimes wet wether. Bring layers of clothes that can be peeled off. A rain poncho also makes a good ground cloth.

Sleeping bag—Select a warm one for cold nights yet lightweight for carrying.

Tent—Synthetic fabrics have made possible a variety of lightweight trail tents, although some hikers get along well with a tarpaulin as a simple shelter. A hammock can serve instead of a tent.

Food—Freeze-dried and dehydrated foods are light to carry and have revolutionized menus in the backcountry. No more hardtack and raisins; now you can turn out miracle meals fit for a king of the trail. From April to October, camping supplies are available at various locations in the park. (See Chapter 8.)

Tools of the trade—Items like a backpacker stove, matches, rope, camp knife, flashlight, canteen, and collapsible water container quickly come to mind. Your list will expand to include other necessities, then shrink to exclude luxuries.

First aid—You will want to take along a standard kit for possible on-the-trail treatment.

Emergency equipment—Depending on how deep into the wilderness you plan to go, you may carry along a mirror, a whistle, or other emergency signaling items. In the winter, take additional clothing and rations.

Before you depart, it is a good idea to leave a copy of your planned itinerary, routes, and time of return with your family or a close friend.

WHEN YOU REACH THE PARK

Pick up your free backcountry permit (during daylight hours only) at an entrance station, at a ranger station, at one of the two park visitor centers, or at park headquarters. Ranger stations are located at Front Royal at the northern end of the park; at Matthews Arm, Thornton Gap and Big Meadows; and at Simmons Gap and Rockfish Gap in the southern part of the park. Park headquarters is four miles west of Thornton Gap on U.S. Highway 211.

PERMIT

If you wish, you may get your backcountry permit ahead of time. Drop a brief letter to the Superintendent, Shenandoah National Park, Luray, VA 22835 (Attn: Backcountry Permit). Tell him the dates you will be in the park, the number in your party, the location and dates of each overnight camp, and of course your name and address.

Issuing backcountry permits allows the park staff to monitor and regulate the number of users in wilderness areas. Permits are an important management tool in the park's plan of dispersed backcountry use.

At several ranger stations, wilderness hikers may view a five-minute slide talk "Backpacking in Shenandoah—What You'll Need To Know." A ranger will be on duty to answer questions concerning trail conditions, weather forecasts, and interesting spots and hazards along the route.

You might also pick up a park minifolder that gives an overall map of the park, as well as another pocket-sized folder titled "Bear—Friend or Foe?"

With your permit, you and your party (maximum of 10 persons) may camp at nearly any isolated location you choose.

BACKCOUNTRY RULES

Now that you are fully equipped and well prepared, there are 190,000 acres open to camping in the Park. Here are the common sense rules governing camping in the backcountry of Shenandoah National Park that the rangers will enforce:

**Permits are required and must be obtained before entering the backcountry.

**Backcountry camping is literally "out of sight!" Pitch your camp at least 250 yards away from any paved road and half a mile from any developed park area. Fade into the wilderness by camping out of sight of any other camping party, and at least 25 yards from any stream.

**Do not plan to bed down in one of the trail shelters. They are for emergency use only—for first aid or protection in a severe storm. You're prepared to camp in the open—do your thing.

**Wood or charcoal fires are not permitted in the Shenandoah backcountry. Improper wood gathering, fire-blackened rocks, and sterilized soil produce longlasting damage to the environment. Instead, bring along one of the efficient and compact backpacker stoves.

**Do not trench your tent or level off your tent site. Erase all evidence of your campsite when you leave. Treat the natural surroundings as gently as you can.

**Two days is the maximum stay at a backcountry campsite. Move along—so the vegetation can restore itself.

**Bearproof your campsite. Hang your food at a distance from your campsite and at least 10 feet above the ground. Choose a limb that cannot support a bear's weight; rig your food above the ground between two trees.

**Lighten your pack by leaving glass containers at home—they are prohibited in the backcountry.

**Horses must be tied near the trailside on a short tether. Free grazing is not permitted. Carry pellet feed for your horse.

**Riders must keep their mounts off foottrails and away from campgrounds and developed areas. Horses may be ridden on designated yellow blazed trails only.

**Pets are best left at home; any pets within the park must be on a short leash, not allowed to run freely.

Violation of backcountry regulations can bring a minimum fine of $25. If you have questions, ask a ranger before you start.

BACKCOUNTRY SANITATION

**Carry out all used cans, aluminum foil and disposables. (Empty cans are easier to carry if you flatten them.) Burying such trash is not satisfactory because it does not decompose and eventually comes to the surface through animal or frost action.

**Place all other refuse in plastic bags and pack it out; don't litter the landscape.

**To insure safe drinking water boil the water for ten minutes.

**After washing dishes or bathing, discard the water and detergent at least 30 feet away from any stream or spring. In this way, the earth will strain the chemicals and prevent steam pollution.

**A small hole should be dug to deposit human waste and covered.

BACKCOUNTRY TRAIL TIPS

**Stay on blazed trails unless you're proficient with your topographical map and compass.

**Team up with one or more companions for safety and comradeship.

**Children—if you have them along, be sure they have identification on them at all times; tell them what to do if they get lost ("stay where you are"); and give them a whistle to signal for help.

**Sign up at trail registers. It's a good safety measure and your information may help park managers learn more about backcountry use.

**In a lightning storm, move downhill below a ridge or a peak. Avoid exposed solitary objects such as large rocks or trees. Find shelter in lower areas, in a dense stand of trees, or under overhanging rocks.

**Limit the weight of your pack to one-fifth your own weight—until you prove you can carry more.

**Never take short cuts across switchbacks in the trail. It can be hazardous for you, can damage the vegetation, and will cause soil erosion.

LAST WORD

Shenandoah's wilderness areas have been set aside as an outdoor museum of natural history. Man, as the intruder, should neither harm nor disturb the natural environment. By preparing for your backcountry visit and by exercising "good mountain manners," you will reserve the wilderness for those who come down the trail after you.

CHAPTER 7
THE TROUT STREAMS

A Message From The Superintendent of Shenandoah National Park

Shenandoah National Park offers one of the few large areas of wild trout habitat in the eastern United States. Each year millions of Americans visit this great national park seeking a chance to enjoy its many natural and cultural resources. Located only a short distance from the nation's capital and other large metropolitan areas Shenandoah provides opportunitites for many people. At the same time, management challenges in the protection of these resources sought after by so many are ever present.

Wild brook trout are but one of the outstanding natural resources we as park managers are charged with protecting. However, it is important to mention that game fish are the only species of wildlife in the Park that, by law, visitors are allowed to harvest or even disturb in any way. Because of this, brook trout populations must be managed carefully in order to assure their long term viability.

The Park's Fisheries Management Plan objectives for native trout management in Shenandoah National Park are twofold: (1) To preserve and perpetuate the native brook trout as an integral component of the Park's aquatic ecosystems and (2) to allow for recreational angling. Meeting these objectives requires careful management and the full cooperation of the angling public. You, as anglers and conservationists, can help to assure that trout populations remain healthy and that the outstanding angling opportunities that now exist continue into the future. Beyond obeying the regulations and being good sports persons, I encourage you, whenever possible, to foster the catch-and-release angling concept, especially in heavily fished streams. This will allow other visitors to have the experience of catching the fish that are released. Handle fish that are to be released carefully to avoid injuring them, and be a good example to other anglers that you encounter on the stream. By doing these things you will have a lasting positive effect on the well being of this precious resource.

If you observe violations of any park regulations, please report your observations to the nearest Ranger station or call Park Headquarters as soon as you can. (703) 999-2227.

My staff and I wish you many memorable outdoor experiences during your visits to the Park, and we hope that you will be able to return often.

* * * * *

The above words from the Park's Superintendent should quicken the heartbeats of all serious trout anglers. Management of the streams to assure the best possible ecosystem for the trout is the finest gift any angler could receive.

Although they have modestly not mentioned it, this is exactly what the officials of the Shenandoah National Park have wisely done ever since the Park was formed over fifty years ago. Judging from this track record, and the cares and concerns I know these individuals have today, I am very optimistic in believing my grandchildren will be able to enjoy the fine brook trout fishing in the Park that I have experienced.

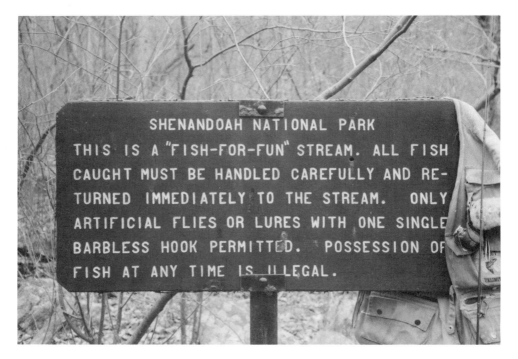

Many serious anglers follow the above creed, even when the regulations do not require it, feeling that **the Park's trout are too valuable to be caught only once.**

In order to protect this delicate resource, Park officials continually monitor all possible influencing factors. During periods of low rainfall, it is sometimes necessary to close certain streams to fishing in order to protect the trout. Angling pressure is watched closely in order to evaluate its effect upon the trout. A drastic change here may result in regulation changes in order to protect the trout.

There are presently three Fish-For-Fun streams in the Park—see these special regulations at the end of this chapter. The rest of the legal trout streams are managed under a uniform system of regulations. However, this may change as Park officials perceive a need. Current fishing regulations can be obtained from ranger stations, entrance locations, and from Park Headquarters.

* * * * *

What can *you* do to help assure this outstanding fishery will continue?

First, you should realize that you have the capacity to adversely affect the trout you are so fond of. Certainly, you would not do this intentionally, but often subtle acts can have far-reaching influences.

In order for the trout to maintain a good population, with the existing fishing pressure, it is imperative that they be handled properly as you release them back into the stream.

- Do not fight them any longer than necessary to bring them in safely.
- Do not squeeze them tightly as you hold them.
- Do not get your fingers in their gills.
- Do not keep them out of the water any longer than necessary.
- Do not slide them around on dry rocks or gravel.
- Do not release them into heavy water which could wash them into boulders and kill them.
- Do not permit them to become entwined in the mesh of a landing net, causing gills, gill cover, and fin damage.
- Gently ease each trout back into the stream in a protected area where he can reach the main pool.

The use of barbless hooks will simplify many of the above problems. Some hooks are made barbless, but it is a simple matter to mash down the barbs of the small hooks used in the Park with needle nose pliers.

Just prior to spawning season in the fall, a trout should be released back into the same pool from which he came. He and his partner may have moved into that pool specifically to spawn, and if the water is low, possibly he would not be able to get back into that pool if released a pool or two lower.

In this same respect, I have often seen trout locked into specific pools in the fall by all sorts of man-made dams. I realize some of the piled-up-stone-dams are constructed by swimmers seeking deeper pools during the summer, but some are constructed by well-meaning, poorly informed anglers attempting to "fix things." Regardless of the intention this can restrict the trout's movements. When this happens they will often attempt to spawn wherever they are.

"In order for the trout to maintain a good population with the existing fishing pressure, it is imperative that they be handled properly as you release them back into the stream." Not only does their future depend on this, but so does yours!

Just last fall I watched two beautiful brookies holding over a solid ledge as the female attempted, in vain, to sweep it suitable for spawning. I removed some stones from the neat little dam someone had constructed. A week later when I was on the stream, the trout had moved down into the next pool and had built a beautiful bed to help replenish the stream. It's hard to tell how many future trout this one little dam could have cost this stream.

After the trout have spawned, use extra care not to wade through the spawning beds. These are very easy to see for several weeks, but gradually they take on the coloration of the rest of the bottom. However, by carefully scanning a pool, you can locate the beds and move around them.

Any violation of the fishing regulations should be reported promptly to a Park Ranger.

Lastly, **practice no kill trout fishing.**

* * * * *

80

Stream Locations

The list of legally fishable streams will be provided each year by Park Officials. These streams are all open to public fishing and can be reached from various locations **within the Park.**

Some of the streams can be reached from outside the Park's boundaries; however, in many cases privately owned land prevents access at the lower reaches of the stream. If lower stream access is not covered on a specific stream, there is either no access, or questionable access to that area. **Do not trespass on private land!!**

As of this writing, the avenues of access listed below are all legal. However, if you have reason to suspect land changes or other factors may have altered this, please contact a Park ranger before proceeding.

All stream accesses are keyed to the PATC maps (sources at the end of this chapter), and having these maps is strongly recommended before going into the Park's backcountry. In some cases the trails are lightly used and can be difficult to follow without these maps. In other cases several trails can cross, and it is easy to get on the wrong trail and end up at the wrong place. In one case, and to a slight extent in two others, there is *no trail*. One would be very foolish to attempt to fish these streams without maps.

The following streams are listed alphabetically with a few minor exceptions which will be self-explanatory.

The milepost marker's, numbered from north to south, are at one mile intervals along the Skyline Drive, and are clearly visible. The trail heads are marked with concrete posts on which metal bands give clear directions and distances for specific trails.

Big Run

There are two trails into Big Run from the Skyline Drive.

The easiest access, although the pull is far from easy, is to park at Doyles River Parking on the east side of the Skyline Drive just south of Milepost 81. From the Big Run Overlook take the Big Run Loop Trail, which connects with the Big Run Portal Trail 2.2 miles down the mountain. The stream is quite small here so you will probably want to hike down this trail toward Rocky Mountain Run.

There is good fishing in Big Run throughout this area, and little Eppert Hollow Run, although it is not very long, is well worth fishing.

Rocky Mountain Run offers good action, especially down close to where it joins Big Run.

81

The upper half of Big Run has better fishing than the lower half. The lower section contains some very large pools, but due to scouring this stream received from a potent hurricane a number of years ago, this area lacks good cover in the pools for the trout.

Big Run has always suffered badly in periods of low rainfall, especially if several such seasons occurred in succession.

I have seen long sections of Big Run completely dry in August, and found the surviving fish locked into isolated pools further upstream—this is when the stream should not be fished. **However,** the stream has always come back well after a few years of good rains. I feel the criticisms I've heard concerning the fishing in this stream in the mid to late 80's are primarily attributable to the low overall annual precipitation in this area.

Big Run is a fine stream, and with a few years of good water levels, it will produce excellent angling.

The second access point is from Brown Mountain Overlook at Milepost 77. Take the Brown Mountain Trail down 0.7 miles to the Rocky Mountain Run Trail, and follow this 2.7 miles down to Big Run. The upper section of this trail is *very steep,* making a long, tough pull back after fishing all day.

Fishing Big Run should definitely be looked on as a rugged wilderness trek, not to be attempted with little thought, nor if you are not in good physical condition. Consider packing in to make the best use of your time and to break up the hike.

Brokenback Run

Access is best from the lower Park boundary by coming in Route 600. Park either at the Old Rag Parking area or pull off beside the Nicholson Hollow Trail. The Weakley Hollow Fire Road follows the stream up to the Corbin Hollow Trail, which parallels the stream in the upper section.

This is a rich stream, and the trout show rapid growth. This produces excellent dry fly action throughout much of the season. However, some of the deep pools will yield their largest trout to large nymphs fished upstream dead drift. The abundance of Blacknose Dace minnows in this stream is your cue to try a few deeply sunken streamers in some of these deep pools.

Cedar Run

The lower Park boundary provides the best access to this stream. Route 600 leads to the upper parking area. Take the White Oak Trail 0.1 mile west to the Cedar Run Trail which is the first trail to the left after crossing the metal bridge. This trail follows the stream.

This is an excellent little stream with lots of good cover for the trout. The deep pools add a special flavor to this stream keeping the trout from being extremely wary during the low water conditions of late summer.

Ants and Beetles fished on 6X tippets with light-line rods are very effective when fished adjacent to the large boulders.

This stream usually provides excellent reproduction for the trout and a good even size distribution. Locally heavy angling pressure exists, but the stream holds its own.

Conway River

This stream flows in and out of the Park, but since the state portion is managed the same as the Park's streams, I'm including it here.

Route 667 through Fletcher is the main access. Drive up to the ford and park on the north side of the stream where you will not block traffic or interfere with private land owners. The ford is very rough most of the time so it is best not to tempt your luck.

The Conway River Road follows the stream for its full length providing easy hiking access.

The alternate way into the Conway is by Route 662 and 615 across a sometimes very rough road. Going in is not too bad, but one wet spring day I was very concerned about getting back up that mountain road. I was afraid I might have to stay in there and fish until the road dried out several weeks later. This road hits the stream only a short distance above where you can reach via 667 so you really don't gain much.

This is a very nice stream—it suffers a little in low water conditions, but is well worth fishing.

A series of rather unfortunate events that occurred one fall, when Gerald Racey and I were fishing this stream, will let you understand our respect for the Conway.

I accidentlaly forgot my hippers and decided I'd just wear tennis shoes and work along the sides of the stream. This lasted for about two pools before I ended up wading wet in deep water and getting thoroughly chilled in 42 degree water.

Later that day, while making some pictures of Gerald fishing, I stepped on the tip of my fly rod and broke off the top six inches, which really hampered my accuracy in fly placement.

Upon returning to the car that evening, I realized I had lost my billfold— fortunately an extensive search of the stream bank finally produced the billfold.

Driving home that evening we had some good chuckles over all these misfortunes. However, to put everything in its proper order of priorities, I laughed and said, "But, I'd do it all again for that kind of fishing."

East Branch Naked Creek

The best access to this stream is from the Naked Creek Overlook just south of Milepost 53 on the western side of the Skyline Drive.

There is no trail down to this stream! However, locating it is not a serious problem; finding your way back out can be. Definitely have your map and compass when you fish this stream.

From the overlook, hike down the left side of the grassy area past the tree line. Swinging left and down the mountain, you may be able to locate an old trail, but don't depend on it. You will find a hollow which leads down to the stream. Though rugged, this is one of the most beautiful parts of the Park.

You are now on the stream in its very upper reaches; the best fishing is downstream. An old wagon road roughly follows down the stream, but it is very hard to see in some areas. Even where you can locate it, the going is tough.

Before heading down the mountain, turn around and take your bearings on what the terrain looks like, so you'll know where to leave the stream and exactly the course you'll need to get back up to your car. Things will look differently when you are hiking back up the mountain than they do going down.

The Park's streams provide many waterfalls in various sizes. These are truly beautiful, and they add to the overall angling experience.

The fishing is good all the way to the lower park boundary. There is a broad variety of water-types, so pick what you like best. Hike down, and fish back up, but don't stay too late and lose your way out.

East Hawksbill Creek

The best access to this stream is from the Hawksbill Gap parking area, about half way between Milepost 45 and 46 at lower Hawksbill Trail head on the west side of the Skyline Drive. You must be very careful, since there are two trails leaving this parking area; the most apparent, and heavily used, trail is the one identified as the Hawksbill Trail on the concrete post. *Do not take this trail.* The trail you want is about twenty feet to the right of the above trail, and is actually a connector of about two hundred feet to the Appalachian Trail.

Directly across the Appalachian Trail is an old wagon road. This is faintly marked with old yellow blaze markings. Both the wagon road and the blazes are difficult to see in some areas so you must be observant. Follow the old road down to the spring and then on down to the stream.

As you would suspect from this access, the stream receives little pressure. The flow is small in the upper reaches, but a short distance below the falls, feeders enter from each side of the stream improving the water level. Don't be too concerned about the silt you see in the upper part of the stream; this is not present in the lower area.

A good way to fish this stream is to hike down toward the lower Park boundary, and fish your way back upstream.

You should definitely have the central section of the Park maps when fishing this stream.

East Swift Run

This stream is easily accessible from Route 33 on the eastern side of the Skyline Drive. There is ample parking just inside the lower Park boundary. The stream lies just to the south side of the road. You can fish up the stream as far as you like, get out on Route 33, and walk back down to your car.

This is a small stream and the easy access puts all the fishermen on this stream it can handle. There is usually good reproduction and carry-over of the small fish, but most of the large fish quickly find their way into someone's creel.

85

Hogcamp Branch

The quickest access to this stream, which is a feeder to the Rose River, is by parking at Dark Hollow Falls parking area. This is located between Milepost 50 and 51 on the eastern side of the drive. Hiking down the Dark Hollow Falls Trail puts you right on the stream.

An alternate approach is from the parking area at Fisher Gap just south of Milepost 49. Hike down the Rose River Fire Road until you cross the stream. Just across the stream the trail leaves the fire road and follows the stream down to where it joins the Rose River—about a mile.

This is a nice stream, but due to its easy access from the drive it receives heavy angling pressure.

Hughes River

The top of this stream can be reached from two different trails.

The Corbin Cabin Cutoff Trail provides good access if you park at the Shaver Hollow parking area just north of Milepost 38. This trail meets the Nicholson Hollow Trail 1.4 miles down the mountain. The latter trail parallels the stream to the lower park boundary.

You can also park at Stony Man Overlook between Milepost 38 and 39. About one hundred yards north is the head of the Nicholson Hollow Trail. Follow this 1.8 miles down to the stream. This is the easiest trail back out.

There is also access at the lower Park boundary. Take Route 600 from Nethers past the bus parking lot for Old Rag Mountain. About a half mile on the right is a small parking area. Take the Nicholson Hollow Trail up into the Park.

The trail along the stream is good, and until the day William Downey and I lost it, I thought it was clearly visible for its entire length.

After fishing some of the lower part of the stream, we decided to get out and hike upstream on the trail to try the upper reaches. We knew the trail paralleled the stream on the right side in that section, but we didn't know how far it was from the stream—most of these trails zigzag up the mountain.

Coming from the stream we somehow crossed the trail without seeing it. After a very long, hard climb through a terrible laurel-boulder-snaky looking mountain side, we realized something was wrong. Once we hiked back down to the stream, we found the trail right beside it. To this day I can't figure out how we missed it.

The Hughes fishes well with dry mayfly imitations, such as the Mr. Rapidan and Light Cahill in sizes 12, 14, and 16 until about mid-June when Dry Black Ants and Crowe Beetles in sizes 16, 18, and 20 are best.

Hannah Run

This is actually a major feeder to the Hughes River, just discussed, and the access is the same. Hannah enters the north side of the Hughes River 1.9 miles up the Nicholson Hollow Trail from the parking area on Route 600.

The tactics used on this stream are much like those used on the Hughes. The water volume is less on Hannah so you may want to gear down a little in tackle, and approach the pools more cautiously.

Ivy Creek

Before telling you how to get in to this stream, I must tell you not to try it without a map and a compass, especially on your first trip. In fact, one Park Ranger encourages that only those anglers "experienced in rugged backcountry conditions" fish this stream.

Why all the concern? Because the terrain is very steep, and in some areas there is no trail.

Now that you've been warned, I'll tell you the two ways to get to the stream.

The easiest way to find the stream, or I should say find your way back out of the stream at the end of the day (Did I spook you?) is to park at Loft Mountain Wayside, a short distance south of Milepost 79. Walk north about one hundred yards to the road on the east side of the mountain which leads to the Ivy Creek maintenance hut—don't park on this road. Follow this trail down to the maintenance hut, and then over to the Appalachian Trail. Follow the Appalachian Trail north to where it crosses the stream, and follow the stream down the mountain. Hike down as far as you like; then fish your way back up. The absence of good trails requires that you use the stream as your guide when coming back up the mountain until you reach the Appalachian Trail.

The alternate access is at Pinefield Gap. Park at the gate just south of Milepost 75 and walk north about one hundred yards to the Appalachian Trail. Take this trail east down to Pinefield Hut. From here, down to the stream, you must follow this drainage hollow. No problem going down, but you could easily miss the hollow when you plan to head out since there is no good trail.

This stream supports a good trout population throughout the entire drainage, even in the upper section, though there is less flow in this area. There are some right deep pools which produce best with nymphs. But, other than these, the whole stream can be fished successfully with dry flies most of the year.

Jeremy's Run

Access to this stream is from the lower side of the Elkwallow Picnic area at Milepost 24. Park in the second parking area, and take the connecting trail for less than one hundred yards to the Appalachian Trail. This trail meets the Jeremy's Run Trail in a short distance, where the former makes a sharp turn to the left. The Jeremy's Run Trail follows the stream its full length.

Portions of this stream go dry during years of little precipitation, and the snakes really work on the trout as the water levels in the pools drop. One fishing these areas the next spring, when the water level is good, will find the fish few and far between. Only after the water has been up for a good while, or after a mini-spring-flood, will other fish move into these previously dry areas.

This is a nice little stream, but it receives very heavy fishing pressure. I feel the explanation for this excessive pressure is that many of the anglers just do not know how to access many of the other Park streams.

Little Hawksbill Creek

This stream is best reached by taking Route 611 east of Stanley. Park fifty yards west of the locked gate and hike about fifty yards south (to your right) to the stream.

This stream receives light angling pressure, possibly due to the fact that there is not a good trail all along its length. The terrain is rugged, but some anglers feel the fishing justifies the effort.

Excellent cover enables these trout to withstand extreme conditions which adversely affect trout in some other streams. One almost invariably sees many young fish, attesting to this excellent cover as well as to good spawning conditions.

The thick overhead canopy is your signal to reach for terrestrial fly patterns. Ants, Beetles, Inchworms, and Crickets are all effective flies on this stream; use sizes 12 and 14 early in the season, and drop down to sizes 16, 18 and 20 by mid-summer.

Madison Run

Access to the lower Park boundary can be gained by parking on Route 708 and hiking up the Madison Run Road. Top access is available by parking at the Browns Gap parking area at Milepost 83 on the western side of the Skyline Drive. Hike down the Madison Run Road. Since the stream flow is small up high and it's about a four mile hike down to good water most anglers go in at the lower Park boundary.

This is a small stream and it gets very low during the summer. The best fishing occurs during the first two months of the season.

Meadow Run

Many anglers know this stream as Riprap. Due to recent land sales outside the lower Park boundary, rangers suggest anglers access this stream from one of the two points on the Skyline Drive.

The best access is from the Wildcat Ridge Parking area just south of Milepost 92. Hike down the Wildcat Ridge Trail 2.7 miles to Riprap Trail which follows the stream. There is good fishing both above and below this point.

Another access point is from the Riprap Trail parking area at Milepost 90. A seventy foot connector trail takes you to the Appalachian Trail which meets Riprap Trail in 0.4 miles. Follow Riprap Trail down to the stream. The best water is about three miles down the mountain from this parking area.

This stream has always appeared to be short on aquatic insects. Even though there are a fair number of Blacknose Dace minnows, the trout don't seem to grow very fast. The young, and even the two year old trout in this stream are smaller than the same age fish in other Park streams.

There is good cover in the stream, especially in the upper section.

Terrestrial fly patterns are very effective, apparently, since the trout are conditioned to living on real land born insects.

This stream gets very low late in the summer, so the earlier you can fish it the better.

North Fork Moormans River

This stream is presently managed as a "Fish-For-Fun" stream in which no trout can be killed, and barbless hooks are required—see the complete special regulations at the end of this chapter.

Access to the lower Park boundary is available from Route 614, which is also known as the Sugar Hollow Road. Park at the upper end of the reservoir and follow this same road up along the stream through the Park gate.

The top of the stream is accessed by parking at the Blackrock Gap parking lot just south of Milepost 87. Walk across the Skyline Drive and hike down the North Fork Moormans River Road. There is some private land along the road and the stream, but it is okay to hike and fish in this area.

The private land is used for grazing cattle so do not drink the water. In fact, do not drink water from *any* Park streams without boiling it ten minutes.

The cover, food, and fishing are better in the upper half of this stream than in the lower half. The upper section provides excellent fish cover with deep pools, large boulders, and well-oxygenated water. The lower section has much less gradient, and even though some of the pools are large, they are silty and don't provide the cover you'll see further upstream.

I'll never forget the first time I fished the upper section of this stream one beautiful, early spring day; realizing I was in private farming land, I wasn't surprised at the sound of someone starting a John Deere tractor. The stream-muffled pup-pup-pup was familiar from a summer of working on a farm as a youngster. I just couldn't understand why, once he got it going, he let it die out—over and over again. A little later my fishing partner, William Downey, caught up with me, and with an excited voice inquired, "Have you heard those ruffed grouse drumming?" Only then did I realize what I thought was a tractor was actually drumming grouse. My Brittany would have been ashamed of me!

Paine Run

Bottom access is good on this stream by parking on Route 661 and hiking up Paine Run Trail. At the top you can park at Blackrock Gap parking lot south of Milepost 87, and follow the above trail down the stream. From this point it is only 3.7 miles to the lower Park boundary, and the trail follows the stream affording good access.

This is a small drainage and a small stream. However, one day this worked to our advantage. Upon discovering another Park stream was too high to fish, my fishing partner for the day, David McCormick of Utah, suggested we try Paine Run. This turned out to be an excellent choice. We caught lots of nice trout. The little extra water in the stream helped hide our approach, and the trout raised readily to large drys.

The best fishing is in the upper two-thirds of the stream, but since it is so small most anglers just start down low and fish their way upstream.

This stream gets very low late in the summer, so fish it in the spring and early summer.

Pass Run

This is a tiny stream. It is easily accessible by taking the first road to the south off Route 211 just inside the uppermost Park boundary on the west side of the mountain. Park close to where this road crosses the stream and fish upstream. The good cover is sparse and so are the fish. But, if you want a challenge this may be your game.

Piney River

This stream is accessible from the top by parking at the Piney River Ranger Station just south of Milepost 22. Hike past the residential trailers, and go down the Range View Cabin Road to where the Piney Branch Trail leads off to the left. This last trail follows the stream to the bottom of the mountain.

There is also bottom access from Route 600. Parking is a problem here; there is room along Route 600 just east of 653 for one or two cars. Please do not block any of the private roads in this area. There is no Park land in this immediate area. Hike up the trail to the Park boundary and gate before you start fishing.

The gradient on this stream varies greatly so explore it, and fish what you like. There is good access with the trail close to the stream in most areas.

One late summer day when this stream was very low, I think I saw more snakes in the pools after the trout than there were trout in the pools.

Pocosin River

This stream is accessible from the Skyline Drive by parking in the area for the Pocosin Cabin, halfway between Milepost 59 and 60. Hike down the Pocosin Fire Road until you come to the Pocosin Hollow Trail, take this to your left, and it leads you to the stream.

This is not a large stream, but I've always felt it is one of the prettiest in the Park.

There is plenty of close overhead tree cover so this would be the stream to use your favorite *short* fly rod.

Rapidan River

Routes 649/670 from Criglersville provide access to the central part of this stream, and Route 662 from Graves Mill provides access to the lower part of the stream. There is a bad ford connecting these two sections, and you are a long way from civilization and telephones if you get stuck and need to be towed out, as I did.

The stream receives very heavy angling pressure, in spite of the bad roads decorated with tail pipes and mufflers.

The whole drainage is managed as a Fish-For-Fun stream. (See these regulations at the end of this chapter.)

President Hoover's Camp is located about a mile and a half above the locked gate on the Rapidan Road.

Drys, nymphs, and streamers are all effective on this stream at various times; however, like most Park streams this can get very low late in the summer. I have seen it so low that it was impossible to get close enough to fish without scaring the trout.

This is the stream after which I named the Mr. Rapidan Dry fly. This fly, in sizes 12 through 18, is an exceptionally good fly on this stream.

Rose River

Top access is available by parking at the Fishers Gap parking area just south of Milepost 49 and hiking down the Rose River Fire Road, which follows the lower two-thirds of the stream to the lower Park boundary. An alternate trail to the uppermost part of the river is available by parking at the above area, but shortly after starting down the mountain on the Rose River Fire Road take the Rose River Loop Trail to your left. The first 0.5 mile of this trail is blazed yellow since it also functions as a horse trail. One half mile down the trail take a blue blazed trail to your right for another 0.5 mile to the stream.

Top access can also be gained by parking at the Dark Hollow Falls parking area and following the Dark Hollow Falls Trail down to the Rose River Fire Road and then following the fire road down to the river. This road has many cut backs, and in some areas it is far from the stream. In these areas there is no good trail close to the stream. You keep your bearings by knowing the road is "up there somewhere" and that the stream is "down there somewhere."

This is where we ran into, almost literally, the rattlesnake which my fishing partner, William Downey, with forty years experience in these mountains, refers to as "the largest rattler" he's ever seen out of captivity.

There is bottom access from Route 670. Things are a little cramped here, so use care not to block the road, preventing its use by Park Rangers.

The fire road is fairly close to the stream for several miles in the lower section before it starts zigzagging.

This is a nice stream with good action on dry flies to mayfly, caddisfly, and stonefly hatches until mid-June; after this, the trout keep looking up for terrestrials.

South River

This stream can be reached by parking at the lower part of the South River Picnic Area between Milepost 62 and 63 on the Skyline Drive. Hike down the South River Falls Trail to the stream.

This is a small stream with only a short section of good water. The scenery is very attractive, so if you can blend the two you can have a good time on this stream.

Staunton River

This is a feeder to the Rapidan River, and it can be reached by Route 662 from Graves Mill. The road gets *very rough* shortly before reaching the stream, so when your car and your kidneys have taken all you feel they can withstand, pull over to the side and park; then walk the rest of the way to the stream.

This stream is managed as a Fish-For-Fun fishery requiring that no fish be killed. (See these regulations at the end of this chapter.)

This is a very small stream, but it's very pretty.

Thornton River, North Fork

Route 612 provides access to the lower portion of this stream. This road is used by residents with homes in this area, so do not block the road. Be willing to park east of the houses and walk in. Hike up the Thornton Hollow Trail into the Park, and you can drop in and fish the stream wherever you like.

There is access into the head of this stream via the Thornton Hollow Trail, which leaves the Skyline Drive halfway between Mileposts 25 and 26. The stream is small here, but hiking down the mountain will get you into more water.

This is a good little stream with a fair trout population. It is one of the northernmost stream on the eastern side of the Park so naturally it gets a fair amount of pressure from anglers in that area.

If your heart is really set on seeing the much-loved Green Drake Mayflies, this stream will give you a chance. Please don't blink, or you may miss all three of them that come off in that specific year.

Thornton River, South Fork

This stream is easily accessible from Route 211 with adequate parking at the lower Park boundary, and at the Buck Hollow Trail parking area about a mile inside the lower Park boundary.

This is a good small stream, but the ease of access keeps the big fish skimmed off. Even considering this, it is well worth fishing.

If you get lost on this stream, it's because you want to.

West Branch Naked Creek

There is good access to the bottom of this stream by coming in Route 607 and parking at the wide area at the end of the road.

There is excellent cover in the upper reaches of this stream, but, naturally, when you get this far up in the mountains, the flow is small.

An angling friend thinks this is one of the best small streams in the Park, and he hasn't missed fishing many of them.

The extreme upstream portion of this stream is in private land, and it receives much pressure there.

Your best angling will come in April and May before the water level drops.

White Oak Canyon Run

A stream with a name this exciting is an appropriate way to end this chapter. The real beauty and grandeur of the stream, itself, is every bit as striking as its name.

The many beautiful waterfalls, the inspiring scenery and the good trout fishing, all make this a stream worth visiting.

The top access is by parking at Limberlost, just east of the Skyline Drive at Milepost 43. Hike 0.1 mile down Old Rag Fire Road to White Oak Canyon Trail. Follow this trail to the right, and it takes you down to the stream, providing good stream access all the way to the bottom of the mountain.

Route 600 provides good access to the lower part of the stream. Park in the area beside the stream and follow White Oak Canyon Trail up along the stream.

There are a number of exciting things about fishing this stream, as there are all of the Park's streams, which I'll leave for you to discover on your own. A large part of the fascination of these streams is the individual personality they develop as you come to know each one. It would be meaningless, and a disservice, for me to attempt to reveal these hidden characteristics of endearment and challenge. What I see, you may not see, and you may see much more than I.

Angling in the Shenandoah National Park is more than catching beautiful wild trout, more than inhaling its striking beauty, more than sinking into its peaceful solitude; it is a filling, of a previously undetected void, with an emotion of complete satisfaction that only God can give.

Fish-For-Fun Regulations

(1) Fishing is restricted to artificial flies or lures with one barbless hook.

(2) No trout of any size may be in possession at any time. All trout caught must be carefully handled and immediately returned to the stream. All other species of game fish may be kept. The creel limit for species other than trout shall be the same as on adjacent State waters.

Map Sources for the Shenandoah National Park

Murray's Fly Shop
P.O. Box 156
Edinburg, VA 22824
(703) 984-4212

Shenandoah National History Association
Shenandoah National Park
Rt. 4, Box 348
Luray, VA 22835

CHAPTER 8
PARK FACILITIES AND INFORMATION SOURCES

Overnight Accommodations:
Skyland Lodge
Dining room, tap room, conference hall, mountain craft, horseback riding, children's playground, religious service provided by a Christian ministry, naturalist activities (include conducted hikes and evening programs).

Season: April through November

Milepost: 41.7

Phone: (703) 999-2211 during season months—during December through March call (703) 743-5108.

Big Meadows Lodge
Dining room, tap room, wagon rides, mountain craft shop, children's playground, religious services provided by a Christian ministry, naturalist activities (include conducted hikes and evening programs).

Season: Mid-May through October

Milepost: 51.3—one mile off Drive

Phone: (703) 999-2221 during season months—during November through mid-May (703) 743-5108.

Lewis Mountain Lodge
Cottages (furnished with bathroom, lights, heat, towels, and linen), campstore, laundry, showers, wood, ice.

Season: May through October

Milepost: 57.6

Phone: (703) 999-2255

Information for above lodges:

Check out time is 12:00 noon.

Check in time is approximately 3:00 P.M.

No pets are allowed in the overnight accommodations.

There are no phones in any rooms. A limited number of rooms have television. Public phones and TV lounges are available at each lodge.

For reservations for the above lodges, you may also write ARA Virginia Sky-line Company, Inc., P.O. Box 727, Luray, VA 22835.

Dining:

Panorama Restaurant
Dining room, gift and craft shop
Season: April through November
Milepost: 31.5
Phone: (703) 999-2265

Skyland Lodge Restaurant
Serves breakfast, lunch, and dinner
Season: April through November
Milepost: 41.7

Big Meadows Lodge Restaurant
Serves breakfast, lunch, and dinner
Season: Mid-May through October
Milepost: 51.3—one mile off Drive

Waysides:
A wayside is a store-snack bar with souvenirs and lunch counter.

Elkwallow Wayside
Snack bar, gift shop, service station, grocery store, campers' supplies, wood, and ice.
Season: May through October
Milepost: 24.1

Big Meadows Wayside
Campers' grocery store, campers' supplies, gift shop, restaurant, bicycle rentals, wood, ice, showers, service stations, laundromat.
Season: March through December with a small operation during November, December, and March.
Milepost: 51.2

Lewis Mountain
Gift shop, grocery store, wood, ice, showers, laundry.
Season: May through October
Milepost: 57.5

Loft Mountain Wayside
Gift shop, campers' grocery, campers' supplies, service station, restaurant.
Season: May through October
Milepost: 79.5

Visitors Center:
Dickey Ridge Visitor Center
This attractive building was converted from an abandoned lodge in 1958. Exhibits introduce what you can see and do in the park. Rangers are available to give short talks on the area's history and natural history—a free movie is shown frequently.
Season: From about April 1 through November 1
Milepost: 4.6

Byrd Visitor Center
This facility was built in 1966 and named for Senator Harry F. Byrd, Sr. It contains a museum with exhibits on the people and natural history of Shenandoah National Park and Big Meadows. Ranger conducted hikes and programs are offered during spring, summer, and fall—a free movie is shown regularly.
Season: Open daily from early March through December and an intermittent schedule during January and February.
Milepost: 51

Campgrounds:
The park has four rustic campgrounds with NO hook-ups for electricity, sewage, or water. There's a 14-day total limit between June 1 and October 31. Check headquarters (703) 999-2243 for opening and closing dates.

Mathews Arm Campground
186 tent and trailer sites, sewage disposal station, summer walks, and evening programs offered by rangers (consult campground bulletin boards for times and locations), Traces Nature Trail, NO shower facilities. Nearby: 2 miles from Elkwallow Wayside & Campstore; Piney River Ranger Station is across Drive from campground entrance.
Milepost: 22.2

Big Meadows Campground
225 sites (193 tent-trailer sites, 62 tent sites), reservations through Ticketron May 21 through October 24 (Ticketron dates subject to change without notice), wood, ice, store open in summer, showers, laundry facilities, amphitheater programs in summer, sewage disposal. Nearby: Big meadows Lodge & Wayside, gas, picnic area, Ranger Station, Byrd Visitor Center, Story of the Forest Trail, Ranger conducted activities and programs in spring, summer, and fall. (Check park bulletin boards for times and locations.)
Milepost: 51

Lewis Mountain Campground
32 campsites, picnic area, camp store, showers, laundry facilities, rustic cabins, campfire programs with Rangers (summer).
Milepost: 57.5

Loft Mountain Campground
221 campsites (167 tent-trailer sites, 54 tent sites), showers, laundry facilities, Loft Mountain Wayside and camp store, Deadening Nature Trail, sewage disposal, Ranger activities, and amphitheater programs. (Summer, check park bulletin boards for times and locations.)
Milepost: 79.5

Campground Regulations:
1) Secure all valuables before leaving your campsite. Don't leave your campsite unattended for more than 24 hours. Always leave something at your site to indicate that it is occupied.

2) Quiet hours are between 10 P.M. and 6 A.M. Portable generators must not be run between these hours. Annoying noises should be avoided at all times.

3) Wood that is both down and dead may be used for campfires. Please don't chop any standing tree, alive or dead. Firewood may be bought in the area.

4) Leave your campsite as clean or cleaner than you found it. This discourages wild animals from cleaning up after you, and also provides a nice welcome for the next campers.

5) Pets should be on leashes or physically restrained at all times; this will keep them from straying and becoming lost, also prevents them from being bothered by skunks.

6) Food must be kept in your car or hung in a tree or on a food storage pole (in walk-in sites) when not being eaten or prepared. Skunks, raccoons, and bears are happy to eat your breakfast for you. These wild creatures are protected in this refuge and must not be fed or harmed in any way.

7) Keep all vehicles on paved surface.

Picnic Areas:
These have picnic tables, fireplaces, drinking fountains, and comfort stations.
Dickey Ridge
Milepost: 4.7
Elkwallow
Milepost: 24.1
Pinnacles
Milepost: 36.7
Big Meadows
Milepost: 51.2

Lewis Mountain
Milepost: 57.5
South River
Milepost: 62.8
Loft Mountain
Milepost: 79.5

Other Services:
Naturalist Programs

Naturalist programs, consisting of evening programs, and campfire talks, hikes, and demonstrations are offered at several locations during the summer and at a few sites during spring and fall. Activity schedules are posted on bulletin boards throughout the park and in *Shenandoah Overlook,* a park newspaper that is available free at most visitor contact stations.

Bicycling

There are no exclusive paths or roads. All cycling must be done on the Skyline Drive, on public roads in developed areas, and on short designated hiker/biker paths at Big Meadows. NO riding on backcountry trails.
—Bicyclists 16 years or older entering the Park by bicycle are charged a single entry permit fee.
—During low visibility and the period between sundown and sunup, each bicycle must exhibit a white light on the front and a red light or reflector on the rear.

Horseback Riding

The Skyland Lodge has horseback riding service and stables. Reservations and information can be obtained at the Lodge front office when the stables are closed.

Emergencies

If you need help or first aid, want to report a missing person, or have any emergency of any kind, contact the nearest Ranger at any visitor center, campground, entrance station, or Ranger Station. You could also send another driver—hiker to find a Ranger, ask concession personnel at waysides or lodges to contact a Ranger for you, or call the emergency phone number at headquarters, staffed 24 hours per day: (703) 999-2227. Pay phones are located in developed areas.

Ranger Stations

The Park maintains four Ranger Stations within the Park. They are usually open during normal working hours.

—Piney River-directly across from Mathews Arm Campground entrance at Mile 22.1.

—Big Meadows-located at campground entrance or follow the signs at Mile 51.2.

—Skyland-Mile 41-43.

—Simmons Gap-take road on east side of skyline Drive at Mile 73.2

Fishing License

A state of Virginia license is required. A five day license is available at wayside facilities and camp stores in the Park. Since the fishing regulations can change, get a current copy when you purchase your license.

OUTSIDE THE PARK
Eastern Side of the Shenandoah National Park
(North to South)

Front Royal, VA

Motels/Hotels:

Quality Inn Skyline Drive
10 Commerce Ave.
Front Royal, VA 22630
Phone: (703) 635-3161 or 800-228-5151
Located near north entrance to Skyline Drive, 552 Bypass.
107 rooms, dining room, swimming pool

Pioneer Motel
541 S. Royal Ave.
Front Royal, VA 22630
Phone: (703) 635-4784
Located on US 340 near Skyline Drive and caverns.
28 rooms, pool, A/C, cable color TV w/HBO, refrigerator, oversized beds available, restaurant, and gift shop.

Front Royal Motel
1400 Shenandoah Ave.
Front Royal, VA 22630
Phone: (703) 635-4114 or 800-HBO-ROYAL
Located at the intersection of US 340, 522, & 50 on N. Shenandoah Ave.
Restaurants within walking distance. Large swimming pool, color TV w/cable and HBO.

Scottish Inn
Front Royal, VA 22630
Phone: 800-251-1962 or (703) 636-6168
Located 1½ blocks from north entrance of Skyline Drive on US 340 South
   and SR 55.
A/C, color TV w/HBO, queen beds, restaurants adjacent.

Center City Motel
416 S. Royal Ave.
Front Royal, VA 22630
Phone: (703) 635-4050
Located 2½ blocks from entrance to Skyline Drive and downtown at intersection of Rts. 55 and US 340, convenient to exits of I-66.
14 rooms, cable color TV, A/C, tub/shower, family suites, all rooms ground
   floor, family restaurant adjacent.

Bluemont Inn
Front Royal, VA 22630
Phone: (703) 635-9447
Located at the north end of Front Royal. Take I-81 to I-66 to Rt. 340, 522,
   and 55.
Color cable TV w/HBO, satellite, whirlpool, waterbeds, limited pets.
   Queen and extra long beds, automatic wakeup, four penthouses, free
   continental breakfast, restaurant adjacent.

Restaurants:
Constant Spring Dining Room
413 S. Royal Ave.
Front Royal, VA 22630
Phone: (703) 635-7010
Located in Constant Spring Inn.
Family Style.

My Father's Moustache
Front Royal, VA 22630
Phone: (703) 635-3496
Located in the Victorian Manor House, downtown on US 340 and Rt. 55.
Steaks, seafood, and deli sandwiches.

Royal Oak Restaurant and Lodge
10 Commerce Ave.
Front Royal, VA 22630
Phone: (703) 635-3161
Located at the Quality Inn.
Full family menu.

Bed & Breakfast Inns:
Constant Spring Inn
413 S. Royal Ave.

Front Royal, VA 22630

Phone: (703) 635-7010

Located at intersection of Rt. 340 and Rt. 55. Three blocks to north entrance to Skyline Drive and Shenandoah National Park.

6 double rooms with private bath and 3 suites with private bath, fireplaces, game room.

Alden Inn Bed & Breakfast
Front Royal, VA 22630

Phone: (703) 636-6645

Located near Front Royal. Take I-81 to I-66, 340 south for 3 miles.

4 rooms, A/C, color cable TV in lounge. Beautiful home in downtown Front Royal.

Campgrounds:
Fishnet Campground
P.O. Box 1919

Front Royal, VA 22630

Phone: (703) 636-2961

Located in Front Royal/Winchester area 2 miles from I-66 & Rt. 522 Junction.

125 sites, electric & water, nature trails, swimming, boating, fishing, dump station, LP gas, pets on leash, laundry facilities, open year round for self contained units, all others April through mid-November.

Skyline Ranch Resort Inc.
P.O. Box 393

Front Royal, VA 22630

Phone: (703) 636-6061

Located near Skyline Drive. Take first right pass entrance to Skyline Drive off Rt. 340 south of Front Royal. Right on 619 west, 5 miles to entrance.

90 sites, electric & water, nature trail, recreation building, store, playground, swimming, boating, fishing, dump station, LP gas, pets on leash, laundry facilities, open year round.

Front Royal KOA
Front Royal, VA 22630

Phone: (703) 635-2741

120 trailer/tent sites, water, electric, sewer hook-ups, dumping station, hot showers, laundry, store, LP gas, swimming pool, fishing, playground, volleyball, horse shoes, mini-golf, recreational hall, planned activities, gospel, bluegrass, country music.

Other Attractions
Front Royal Canoe Co.
Front Royal, VA 22630

Phone: (703) 635-5440

Located near Skyline Drive. Take I-66 east to Rt. 340 south, 3 miles past Skyline Drive.

Canoe and tube trips on Shenandoah River which flows north between the Shenandoah National Park and George Washington National Forest.

Skyline Caverns, Inc.
P.O. Box 193

Front Royal, VA 22630

Phone: (703) 635-4545

Located at the beginning of Skyline Drive and Shenandoah National Park at I-81 and I-66.

See thirty million years of breathtaking beauty beneath the earth! Ride a 1/5-scale miniature train.

Open year round.

Warren Rifles Confederate Museum
95 Chester St.

Front Royal, VA 22630

Phone: (703) 636-6982

Relics, weapons, uniforms, and battle flags of the Civil War.

Flint Hill, VA

Restaurants
The Corner Post
Flint Hill, VA 22627

Phone: (703) 675-3862

The Schoolhouse Restaurant
Flint Hill, VA 22627

Phone: (703) 675-3030

Bed & Breakfast Inns
Caledonia Farm Bed & Breakfast
Rt. 1, Box 2080

Flint Hill, VA 22627

Phone: (703) 675-3693

Washington, VA

Motel/Hotel
Black Kettle Motel
Washington, VA 22747
Phone (703) 675-3539

Restaurants
Black Kettle Restaurant
Washington, VA 22747
Phone: (703) 675-3539

Bed & Breakfast Inns
Inn at Little Washington
Washington, VA 22747
Phone: (703) 675-3800
Rates are expensive including full breakfast. Open all year. 8 rooms and 2 penthouse suites w/jacuzzis, restaurant open Wed. through Sun. for dinner only, for guests and public. Children over ten, NO pets.

Foster-Harris House
Main St.
Washington, VA 22747
Phone: (703) 675-3757

Sycamore Hill House
Washington, VA 22747
Phone: (703) 675-3046

Heritage House Bed & Breakfast
P.O. Box 90
Washington, VA 22747
Phone: (703) 675-3738 or (703) 675-3207

Sperryville, VA

Restaurants
Teepee Restaurant
Sperryville, VA 22740
Fast food—lunch and dinner, salad bar, dining room.

Bed & Breakfast Inns
The Conyers House
Slate Mills Rd.
Sperryville, VA 22740
Phone: (703) 987-8025
9 rooms, 3 with private bath. Pets and Children not permitted.

Nethers Mill
Rt. 1, Box 62
Sperryville, VA 22740
Phone: (703) 987-8225

Campgrounds
Piney River Campground
Rt. 1, Box 260
Sperryville, VA 22740
Phone: (703) 987-8766
Located 8 miles east of Skyline Drive on US 211, then 3 miles north on VA 612.
50 sites, electric, nature trails, recreation building, store, playground, fishing, dump station, showers, firewood for sale, pets on leash.
Open April through November (year round with reservations).
Private secluded mountain sites, magnificent scenery, wildlife, direct access to Shenandoah National Park.

Other Attractions
That Sperryville Emporium
Sperryville, VA 22740
Phone: (703) 987-8270
Discount dealers in pottery, furniture, and gifts.
Open year round.

Rainbow Run Trail Rides
Sperryville, VA 22740
Endless mountain trails, riders of all ages, beginner and experienced riders welcomed. Short rides, all day rides. Moonlight and overnights. Open year-round—inexpensive.

Round Hill, VA

Bed & Breakfast Inns
Round Hill Hall
Rt. 7, Box 14
Round Hill, VA 22141
Phone: (703) 338-5331

Boston, VA

Bed & Breakfast Inns
Meadowood
Slate Mills Rd. Rt. 707
Boston, VA 22713
Phone: (703) 547-3851

Syria, VA

Bed & Breakfast Inns
Grave's Mountain Lodge
Rt. 670
Syria, VA 22743
Phone: (703) 923-4231

Culpepper, VA

Motels/Hotels
Holiday Inn
P.O. Box 1286
Culpepper, VA 22701
Phone: (703) 825-1253 or 800-HOLIDAY
Located on Rt. 29 south.

Super 8 Motel
889 Willis Ln.
Culpepper, VA 22701
Phone: (703) 825-8088 or 1-800-843-1991

Comfort Inn
890 Willis Ln.
Culpepper, VA 22701
Phone: (703) 825-4900 or 1-800-228-5150

Econo-Lodge Culpepper
P.O. Box 407
Culpepper, VA 22701
Phone: (703) 825-5097 or 1-800-446-6900
Located on US 15 and US 29 bypass, use Culpepper/Orange exit.
48 rooms, free in-room movies, color TV, free coffee, family and senior
citizens discounts, AAA approved.

Sleepy Hollow Motel
400 James Madison Hwy.
Culpepper, VA 22701
Phone: (703) 825-8396
Located on Rt. 29 and 15 north, in town across from mall.
34 rooms, color TV, direct dial phones, pets accepted.

Restaurants
Aberdeen Barn
Culpepper, VA 22701
Phone: (703) 825-1037
Located on Rt. 29 south next to Holiday Inn.
Open daily. Breakfast, lunch, and dinner featuring steak and seafood.

Hong Kong Restaurant
550 Culpepper Mall
Culpepper, VA 22701
Phone: (703) 825-0158
Authentic chinese food.

The Jade Restaurant
325 Southgate Shopping Center
Culpepper, VA 22701
Phone: (703) 825-3443
Chinese cuisine.

Hung's
900 S. Main St.
Culpepper, VA 22701
Phone: (703) 825-5342

Country Cookin
247 Southgate Shopping Center
Culpepper, VA 22701
Phone: (&03) 825-6565
Steaks and salad bar.

Davis Street Ordinary
195 E. Davis St.
Culpepper, VA 22701
Phone: (703) 825-3909
Fine gourmet food/French cuisine.

Golden Coral
891 Willis Lane
Culpepper, VA 22701
Phone: (703) 825-5888
Located on Rt. 29 south.

Jenner's and Family Restaurant
306 S. Main St.
Culpepper, VA 22701
Phone: (703) 825-4222
Old fashion American diner.

Ciro's Italian Pizzeria & Restaurant
741 Dominion Square Shopping Center
Culpepper, VA 22701
Located on Business 29 north.
New York style pizza, subs, and Italian dinners.

Bed & Breakfast Inns
Fountain Hall Bed & Breakfast Inn
609 S. East St.
Culpepper, VA 22701-3222
Phone: (703) 825-8200
Located approximately 25 miles from Skyline Drive.
Graciously accommodating for business and leisure travelers in historic
   downtown.

Campgrounds
Rolling Acres Campground
Culpepper, VA 22701
Phone: (703) 547-3374 or (703) 547-2354
Located 25 miles from Skyline Drive. From Rt. 29/15 turn east on Rt. 603,
   right on 657, right on 645, left on 752.
Tent/trailer sites (woods or field), tables, fireplace, dumping station, water
   & electric hookups, field for primitive camping, toilets, and hot showers.

Other Attractions
Dominion Wine Cellars
Box 1057
Culpepper, VA 22701
Phone: (703) 825-8772
Located on Rt. 29 bypass at exit of Rts 552/3.
Premium Virginia wines from hand-tended vineyards.

Mt Run & Pelham Lakes

Culpepper, VA 22701

Offers beautiful lakeside parks with picnic, boating, fishing, and other recreational facilities. If hunting and fishing suit your fancy, quail, deer, fox, turkey and dove are abundant. Excellent fishing is available in the Rappahannock and Rapidan Rivers.

Crozet, VA

Campgrounds
Montfair Family Resort

Crozet, VA

Phone: (804) 823-5202

Located 8 miles east of Skyline Drive on US 33, then 20 miles south on VA 810. 68 sites, water, electric, sewage dump station, showers, laundry facilities, firewood for sale, store, playground, lake swimming, horseback riding, tennis. Open all year.

Haywood, VA

Bed & Breakfast Inns
Shenandoah Springs Country Inn

Rt. 609, Box 122

Haywood, VA 22702

Phone: (703) 923-4300

Madison, VA

Bed & Breakfast Inns
Dulaney Hollow Guesthouse

Rt. 231

Madison, VA

Phone: (703) 923-4470

Campgrounds
Shenandoah Hills Campground

Rt. 1, Box 7

Madison, VA 22727

Phone: (703) 948-4186

Located at the foot of the Blue Ridge Mountains and the Shenandoah National Park on Rt. 29.

89 sites, electric, sewer, nature trails, recreation building, store, playground, swimming, dump station, LP gas, pets on leash, laundry. Open year round, reservations accepted.

Standardsville, VA

Bed & Breakfast Inns
Golden Horseshoe Inn
Rt. 33 west
Standardsville, VA 22973
Phone: (703) 690-3377
Located 32 miles from Skyline Drive.
1825 brick colonial fireplaces, jacuzzis, A/C.

Campgrounds
Morning Star Family Campground
Rt. 1, Box 613A
Standardsville, VA 22973
Phone: (804) 985-7022
Located 1½ miles east of Standardsville on Rt. 230.
54 sites, electric, water, nature trail, store, playground, swimming, fishing, dump station, LP gas, pets on leash. Open mid-April through mid-November, reservations accepted.

Western Side of the Shenandoah National Park
(North to South)

Luray, VA

Motels/Hotels
Luray Inn & Conference Center
Rt. 211 E.
Luray, VA 22835
Phone: (703) 743-4521

The Mimslyn Hotel
401 W. Main St.
Luray, VA 22835
Phone: (703) 743-5105
Elegant surroundings, fine food, conference facilities, lounge.

Cardinal Motel
Luray, VA 22835
Phone: (703) 743-5010
Located on US Business 211, 2 miles east of Luray Caverns.
24 rooms, A/C, color cable TV, pets, near restaurants and shopping center.

Hillside Motel
Luray, VA 22835
Phone: (703) 743-6322
Located on US 211 just east of Luray, near Luray Caverns and Skyline Drive.
16 rooms, A/C, pool, TV, pets.

Intown Motel
410 W. Main St.
Luray, VA 22835
Phone: (703) 743-6511
Located on US 211 at 410 W. Main St. ¼ mile east of Luray Caverns.
65 rooms, A/C, pool, free movie channel, king and queen and extra long
  beds available, playground, and cocktail bar.

Luray Caverns Motel East
Luray, VA 22835
Phone: (703) 743-4531
Located on US 211 Business at east entrance to Luray Caverns, opposite
  Luray Singing Towers. 18 hole golf course, 10 minutes from Skyline Drive.
44 rooms including apartment unit, executive suite, A/C, pool, color TV,
  phones, pets.

Restaurants

Brown's Chinese & American Restaurant
3436 W. Main St.
Luray, VA 22835
Phone: (703) 743-5630
Located in downtown Luray.

Dan's Steak House
Phone: (703) 743-6285
Located on US 211 12 miles west of Luray on Massanutten Mountain.

Intown Restaurant
Phone: (703) 743-6511
Located at Intown Motel
Breakfast, lunch, and dinner-steak, seafood.

The Mimslyn Restaurant
Phone: (703) 743-5105
Located on US 211 at the Mimslyn Hotel.
Breakfast, lunch, and dinner, Sunday brunch.

Bed & Breakfast Inns

Boxwood Place
120 High St.
Luray, VA 22835
Phone: (703) 743-4748

Mountain View House
151 S. Court St.
Luray, VA 22835
Phone: (804) 979-7264 or (703) 743-3723

Shenandoah Countryside
Rt. 2, Box 377
Luray, VA 22835
Phone: (703) 743-6434

Shenandoah River Resort
Rt. 3, Box 224-B
Luray, VA 22835
Phone: (703) 743-3467

Campgrounds
Yogi Bear Jellystone Camp Resort
Luray, VA 22835
Phone: (703) 743-4002
Located 5 miles west of Skyline Drive on US 211.
150 sites, water, electric, sewer hookups, sewage dump station, showers, laundry facilities, firewood for sale, store, playground, game room, pool, fishing. Open March through October.

The Country Waye Campground
Luray, VA 22835
Phone: (703) 743-7222
Located 9 miles west of Skyline Drive on US 211, then 2 miles north on US 340 at VA 658 on Pass Run.
57 sites, water, electric, sewer hookups, sewage dump station, showers, laundry facilities, firewood for sale, store, playground, game room, fishing. Open April through mid-November.

Other Attractions
Luray Caverns
Luray, VA 22835
Located on US 211 Bypass, 10 minutes to central entrance of Skyline Drive.
Largest and most popular cave in the East. A feature of the one hour conducted tour is the Great Stalacpipe Organ.

Car & Carriage Caravan
Phone: (703) 743-6551
Located on US 211 Bypass at Luray Caverns.
The collection of 75 antique vehicles includes one of the oldest cars in the country, an 1892 Benz. All the cars in running condition including a 1906 Ford, a 1907 Buick, a 1911 Hupmobile, a 1913 Stanley Steamer, and Rudolph Valentino's 1925 Rolls Royce.

Luray Reptile Center
Located on US 211, ¾ mile west of Caverns.
Virginia's largest reptile collection. Also exotic animals and birds, petting zoo, gift shop.

Zib's Country Collection
Located at 24 East Main Street, Luray. Take exit 67 off I-81 to 211 east.
Antiques, crafts, trains, "Madame Alexander" dolls.

New Market, VA

Motels/Hotels
Quality Inn
New Market, VA 22844
Phone: 800-228-5151
Located right off I-81, Exit 67.
99 rooms, A/C, pool, color TV, free movie channel, sauna, mini-golf, gift
shop.

Battlefield Motel
New Market, VA 22844
Phone: (703) 740-3105
Located on US 11 one mile north of I-81, Exit 67.
14 rooms, A/C, cable color TV, playground, basketball, free coffee, refrig-
erators, phones in room.

Restaurants
Battlefield Family Restaurant
Phone: (703) 740-3664
Located on US 11 one block south of I-81, Exit 67.
Open year round. Home cooking and daily specials. Soup and salad bar.

Southern Kitchen
New Market, VA 22844
Phone: (703) 740-3514
Located on US 11 3 blocks south of I-81, Exit 67.
Steak, VA ham, seafood, fried chicken.

Campgrounds
Endless Caverns Campground
New Market, VA 22844
Phone: (703) 740-3993 or (703) 896-CAVE
Located south of New Market. Take Exit 66 off I-81, US 11 north for 3½ miles
or take Exit 67, US 11 south for 3 miles to Caverns' entrance.
Water, electric hookups, hot showers, flush toilets, fireplaces, pay phones,
gift/snack shop, picnic grounds. Open May through October—self
contained units only after October 1st.

Other Attractions
New Market Battlefield Park
New Market, VA 22844
Phone: (703) 740-3102
Located off I-81, Exit 67.
Non-profit $2 million Civil War museum, covers entire war with artifacts,
displays, exhibits, dioramas, two award-winning motion pictures (Stone-
wall Jackson and VMI Cadets). Park has 260 acres, spectacular overlooks
above Shenandoah River, scenic walking trails, restored 19th century
farm, historic garden, blacksmith shop, loom house, and bake oven.

Endless Caverns
New Market, VA 22844
Phone: (703) 896-CAVE or (703) 740-3993
Located near New Market. From I-81, Exit 66, travel 3½ miles north on US
11 or take Exit 67 and travel 3 miles south on US 11.
Virginia's premier attraction since 1920, features many rooms of live,
exquisite formations displayed in their natural color.

New Market Airport
New Market, VA 22844
Located off I-81, Exit 67.
Plane rides and rental, flight instruction, charter service, picnic grounds.

Stanley, VA

Restaurants
Jordan Hollow Farm Inn Restaurant
Stanley, VA 22851
Phone: (703) 778-2209
Located at Jordan Hollow Farm Inn (listed below).
Breakfast, lunch, and dinner—rib-eye steak, sauteed trout, quail, pork
chops, ham, and broiled chicken breast.

Bed & Breakfast Inns
Jordan Hollow Farm Inn
Rt. 2, P.O. Box 375
Stanley, VA 22851
Phone: (703) 778-2209 or (703) 778-2285
Located about 8 miles from Luray. From Rt. 340, 6 miles south, turn left
onto 624, left on Rt. 689, and right on Rt. 626.
20 rooms with private bath, NO pets allowed.

Shenandoah, VA

Motels/Hotels
Shenandoah Motel
409 Long Ave.
Shenandoah, VA 22849
Phone: (703) 652-6060

Restaurants
Shenandoah Restaurant
409 Long Ave.
Shenandoah, VA 22849
Phone: (703) 652-6060
Located at the Shenandoah Motel.

Elkton, VA

Motels/Hotels
Elkton Motel
Elkton, VA 22827
Phone: (703) 298-1463
Located on US 33 east.

Ski-Haus Motel
Elkton, VA 22827
Phone: (703) 298-8889
Located on US 33 east.

Skyline Ridge Motel
Rt. 3
Elkton, VA 22827
Phone: (703) 298-9677

Restaurants
Ski-Haus Restaurant
Elkton, VA 22827
Phone: (703) 298-8889
Located on Highway 33 east in Ski-Haus Motel.

Bed & Breakfast Inn
Jo Anne's Bed & Breakfast
Rt. 2, Box 276
Elkton, VA 22827
Phone: (703) 298-9723
Located on Rt. 33 east on a farm 3 miles from Massanutten.
Full breakfast, private bath, and entrance.

Campgrounds
Swift Run Campground
Elkton, VA 22827
Phone: (703) 298-8086
Located 4 miles west of Skyline Drive on US 33.
40 sites, water, electric, sewer hookups, sewage dump station, showers, laundry facilities, firewood for sale, store, game room, pool. Open all year.

McGaheysville, VA

Motels/Hotels
Massanutten House Rentals
Mcgaheysville, VA 22840
Phone: (703) 289-9466

Bed & Breakfast Inns
Shenandoah Valley Farm
Rt. 1, Box 142
McGaheysville, VA 22840
Phone: (703) 289-5402 or (703) 896-9702

Grottoes, VA

Other Attractions
Grand Caverns Regional Park
P.O. Box 478
Grottoes, VA 24441
Phone: (703) 249-5705
America's oldest show cave. Renowned for Civil War history and geologic formations. Open April through October and weekends in March.

Waynesboro, VA

Motels/Hotels

Comfort Inn
604 W. Broad St.
Waynesboro, VA 22980
Phone: 800-228-5150 or (703) 942-1171
Located near entrance to Skyline Drive and Blue Ridge Parkway. 2.9 miles north of I-64, Exit 17 and 4 miles west I-64, Exit 19 on Rt. 250-340 bypass.
75 rooms, A/C, pool, cable TV, attractive guest rooms. Restaurant adjacent with 10% discount for all guest meals, children under 16 free.

Delux Motor Court-AAA
Waynesboro, VA 22980
Phone: (703) 949-8453
Located close to Skyline Drive and Blue Ridge Parkway. I-64, Exit 17 to US 340 north to US 250 west or I-81, Exit 57 to US 250 east 7 miles.
25 rooms, A/C, pool, satellite, color TV w/HBO, direct dial phones, some pets, playground.

Red Carpet Inn of Waynesboro
Waynesboro, VA 22980
Phone: (703) 943-1101
Located near entrance to Skyline Drive and Blue Ridge Parkway at junction of I-64 and US 340, Exit 17.
100 rooms, A/C, pool, color TV.

Holiday Inn-Afton Mountain
Phone: (703) 942-5201
Located 5 miles east of Waynesboro, where Skyline Drive meets the Blue Ridge Parkway. I-64, Exit 19.

Best Western Wayne Motor Lodge
640 W. Broad St.
Waynesboro, VA 22980
Phone: (703) 942-1171 or 800-528-1234
Located 3 miles from I-64 on 250 and 340 bypass.
61 rooms, cable TV, pool.

General Wayne Inn
P.O. Box 429
Waynesboro, VA 22980
Phone: (703) 949-8117
Located at 620 W. Main St.
32 rooms, dining room with portable bar.

Restaurants

General Wayne Inn
620 W. Main St.
Waynesboro, VA 22980
Serves breakfast, lunch, and dinner.

Capt'n Sam's Landing
2323 W. Main St.
Waynesboro, VA 22980
Fresh seafood, mixed beverages, children's menu.

Western Sizzlin Steak House
Waynesboro, VA 22980
Phone: (703) 942-5100
Located off I-64 to Rt. 340 Waynesboro exit.

Campgrounds

Waynesboro Campground
Phone: (703) 943-9573
Located 6 miles north of Waynesboro on US 340.
130 sites, water and electric hookups, sewage dump station, showers, laundry facilities, store, game room, pool.

Other Attractions

Shenandoah Valley Art Center
600 W. Main St.
Waynesboro, VA 22980
Phone: (703) 949-7662

Virginia's Metal Crafters Factory Showroom
Waynesboro, VA 22980
Colonial reproductions.

For Additional Information:

Virginia Division of Tourism
202 North Ninth St.
Richmond, VA 23219
Phone: (804) 786-2051 or 1-800-VISITVA

Shenandoah National Park, Skyline Drive
Rt. 4, Box 292
Luray, VA 22835
Phone: (703) 999-2243

Commonwealth Of Virginia (For Maps)
Dept. of Highways and Transportation
1221 East Broad St.
Richmond, VA 23219

The Shenandoah Natural History Assoc.
Shenandoah National Park
Rt. 4, Box 348
Luray, VA 22835

Chamber of Commerce of Front Royal & Warren Co.
P.O. Box 568
Front Royal, VA 22630
Phone: (703) 635-3185

Culpepper Chamber of Commerce
133 W. Davis St.
Culpepper, VA 22701
Phone: (703) 825-8628

Madison Chamber of Commerce
P.O. Box 373
Madison, VA 22727
Phone: (703) 948-4455

Page County Chamber of Commerce
46 E. Main St.
Luray, VA 22835
Phone: (703) 743-3915

Waynesboro-East Augusta Chamber of Commerce
301 W. Main St.
Waynesboro, VA 22980
Phone: (703) 949-8203

Shenandoah Valley Travel Assoc.
New Market, VA 22844
Phone: (703) 740-3132

Murray's Fly Shop
P.O. Box 156
Edinburg, VA 22824
Phone: (703) 984-4212
PATC Maps and fishing information.

INDEX